The
Nerdist
Way

The
Nerdist
Way

HOW TO REACH THE NEXT LEVEL
(IN REAL LIFE)

Chris Hardwick

Berkley Books, New York

THE BERKLEY PUBLISHING GROUP
Published by the Penguin Group
Penguin Group (USA) Inc.
375 Hudson Street, New York, New York 10014, USA

Penguin Group (Canada), 90 Eglinton Avenue East, Suite 700, Toronto, Ontario M4P 2Y3 Canada
(a division of Pearson Penguin Canada Inc.) • Penguin Books Ltd., 80 Strand, London WC2R 0RL,
England • Penguin Group Ireland, 25 St. Stephen's Green, Dublin 2, Ireland (a division of Penguin
Books Ltd. • Penguin Group (Australia), 250 Camberwell Road, Camberwell, Victoria 3124, Australia
(a division of Pearson Australia Group Pty. Ltd.) • Penguin Books India Pvt. Ltd., 11 Community
Centre, Panchsheel Park, New Delhi—110 017, India • Penguin Group (NZ), 67 Apollo Drive,
Rosedale Auckland, 0632, New Zealand (a division of Pearson New Zealand Ltd.) • Penguin Books
(South Africa) (Pty.) Ltd., 24 Sturdee Avenue, Rosebank, Johannesburg 2196, South Africa

Penguin Books Ltd., Registered Offices: 80 Strand, London, WC2R, 0RL England

While the author has made every effort to provide accurate telephone numbers and Internet addresses
at the time of publication, neither the author nor the publisher is responsible for errors, or for
changes that occur after publication. Further, the publisher does not have any control over and
does not assume any responsibility for author or third-party websites or their content.

Neither the publisher nor the author is engaged in rendering professional advice or services to the individual
reader, and neither shall be liable or responsible for any loss or damage allegedly arising from any information
or suggestion in this book. Anyone participating in the activities and exercises that this book discusses or
suggests assumes responsibility for his or her own actions and safety. If you have any health problems or
medical conditions, or any other concerns about whether you are able to participate in any of these activities
and exercises, consult with your physician before undertaking any of them. The information contained in
this guide book cannot replace such professional advice, or sound judgment and good decision making.

PUBLISHING HISTORY
Berkley hardcover edition / November 2011
Berkley trade paperback edition / November 2012

ISBN: 978-0-425-25318-2

The Library of Congress has catalogued the Berkley hardcover edition as follows:

Hardwick, Chris.
The nerdist way : how to reach the next level (in real life) / Chris Hardwick.—1st ed.
           p.   cm.
ISBN 978-0-425-24354-1
1. Geeks (Computer enthusiasts)—Humor. 2. Success—Humor. I. Title.
PN6231.E4H37 2011
818'.602—dc23
2011023831

PRINTED IN THE UNITED STATES OF AMERICA

10   9   8   7   6   5   4   3   2   1

This book is lovingly dedicated to [YOUR NAME], goodly nerd. You know, [YOUR NAME], every day you get out of bed to [THING YOU DO AT WORK OR HOME OR HOME OFFICE] in [YOUR CITY] despite hating it with every fiber of your being. Now that I have your money, I would very much hope that you achieve as much success in your life as [PLEASING SIMILE THAT IS SIGNIFICANT TO YOU IN SOME WAY]. All my heartfelt best to you, [SHORTENED VERSION OF YOUR FIRST NAME]!

CONTENTS

Introduction   ix

PART ONE: MIND

You Own Your Mind   3

RPG Your Life   13

Seize Your Inner Monologue   27

Choo-Choo-Chooooosing   45

Hi, Anxiety!   59

Doctor Xaviering Your Mind   75

Addiction-ary   89

Sucstress   99

PART TWO: BODY

You Start Now   109

The Getting-Off-Your-Butt Part   119

Workouts   131

PART THREE: TIME

Things That Are Bigger Than You   189

Set Up Your Own Post Office: Presort Your Mail   193

Tracking Your Time   199

Become an Evil Genius   213

Tracking Your Finances   219

Use Trashing to Simplify Your Life   233

Learn to Say No (But Not to This Chapter)   239

Build Your Workfolio   243

Recurring Themes of This Book   261

You. Are. Worth. It.   271

Nerdist Origin Story   275

The Thank You Part   283

INTRODUCTION

Nerds. Once a tortured subrace of humans condemned to hiding in dark corners from the brutal hand of social torment . . . now, captains of industry!

The explosive popularity of the Internet, video games, and smartphone technology has made this formerly feeble cluster of pasty virgins "cool." The same jocks/bullies who pushed us around in school now carry around cell phones, have desktops, laptops, a DVR, DSLR cameras, and Xboxes (Xbocies?); they know what "3G" is. The war is over. The Nerds have won. This was no accident. The Nerd uprising can be attributed to an unnatural ability to obsess and focus when others would be content with "letting it go."

If you are a part of now-glamorous Nerd Herd subculture but still feel like you're waiting to claim your gold cup at the top of the social food chain, then I am here to help you. I shall attempt, through the primitive form of communication known as "writing," to help you milk your Nerdy attributes into a delicious and useful pulp. By the end, you will hopefully know more about who you are, why you should be comfortable with that, and how to leverage those attributes into getting the things you want (you will hopefully also figure out what exactly that is). Oh, and achieving happiness. That's kind of a big one, too.

You don't have to be a stereotypical geekwad to give yourself over to the philosophical tenets of Nerdism, the ideology for us obsessive types. All one needs is a willingness to hone his or her innate ability for overanalysis and hyper-self-awareness—A QUALITY NERDS ALREADY POSSESS—and use it for GOOD. Playing Call of Duty for twenty-three hours straight is cool and all, but I'm going to teach you, my fellow Nerds, how to also spend time on things in your life that will get you the following two things: PAID and LAID. (That rhymes, Marge, and YOU KNOW it rhymes.) Or at least better equipped to get out of your own way and be productive with the likely result of the paying and laying thing (which sounded incredibly douchey when I read it back aloud).

SCHWAAA???

There are Nerds, and then there are Nerdists. A Nerdist is, more specifically, an artful Nerd. He or she doesn't just consume, he or she creates and innovates. (Unintentional rhyme this time. ← On purpose that time.) Freelancers, game designers, graphic designers, DMs (Dungeon Masters), musicians, artists, crafties, and writers are all examples of Nerdists. Yes, we obsess over things, but we are also driven to produce stuff. It may not be surprising, then, to hear (with your eyes, since you're reading this) that I refer to Nerdists as "creative obsessives." The technology explosion in the Information Age has allowed us to flourish, whereas even as recently as fifteen years ago we would have had to get jobs that devoured our souls and pooped them out into little cubes, with little recourse for pursuing our Nerdly passions in any professional capacity. OUR TIME IS NOW. It's actually *cool* to be *smart*—REWARDED even! It is a Golden Age for Nerds. It is our time to THRIVE. You can be a *thriver* (even though that word itself creeps me out for some reason)!

As the founder of Nerdism (your new object of worship), I have long been fascinated by productivity and what motivates people to achieve greatness. The Internet is the great equalizer. We all have access to the same data at all times, so there are fewer excuses. How do some people break through while others remain miserable and inert? I ask this question a lot. I have spent even more time trying to ascertain the answer(s).

"Well, who the fuck do you think you are, Chris Hardwick, comedian, former dating show host, current cable host, and podcaster? Why should I listen to even one crappy word you say?" First off, you're very aggressive. Second, good questions. I have been a lifelong Nerd. As a youth, I was a Nerd in the unironic era of the 1980s when it wasn't a cool buzzword yet. Talk of chess club and D&D could get you stuffed in a trash can. Let me rephrase that: One day after chess club, I got stuffed in a trash can. It is this type of experience that motivates the Nerd to utter under his breath while picking pork rinds and banana peels off his short-sleeve button-down, "I'll show you bastards . . . SOMEDAY I'LL SHOW YOU ALL." [crying starts] But, unfortunately, something happens as we relinquish our life reins and get caught up in unhealthy patterns that keep us from "showing them all."

When I was twenty-two, I started working for MTV through

a fluke audition. It was a weird accident, but it launched a better career for me right out of college than I would have had otherwise. At least, it seemed like it was a good thing. Had I been mentally prepared to handle the responsibility it would have been good. The erroneous lesson that I learned was "Work just falls in your lap." Again, if you're prepared for it, that's good. I was not.

What followed were several years of laziness, drinking, and fuckups on my part. This "woo-hoo/par-tay" attitude piloted my brain through my twenties. Then, when I hit thirty, I began to look around at my life: I was consuming a baby elephant's weight in alcohol EVERY DAY. I lived in a shitty apartment near UCLA (where I went to school—apparently I had become the dude who wouldn't leave and bummed out the college partygoers), my place was always a mess, I had ruined my credit, and I had no real work prospects. I had become a thing I had always feared—the fat, drunk guy who used to be on television. Back when I was working on MTV (which, oddly, at one time, aired short films set to popular music), there was sort of a curse that dictated that one might not "hit it any bigger," after his or her time there, as it were. I always recoiled at the thought of this curse, and here I was taking active steps *every fucking day* to make it happen.

Long story not much shorter, I somehow had the good sense to take stock and ask myself what was important. I knew that I had two choices: I could continue living the way I was living or make broad, sweeping changes. I knew the latter at least gave me a prayer of salvaging my life. In the former, I die in an overweight booze-tomb. It occurred to me that I had sent all of the Nerd qualities that defined me as a youth to the attic, like so many old comic books and outdated game consoles. However, I distinctly remembered that I had pretty intense focusing capabilities. Programming computers (in BASIC, no less), winning chess tournaments, playing video games, collecting action figures, playing D&D, ruining bell curves in Latin class . . . there was *something* there that I could use in the present day. Deep down I was still the outcast kid who had decided to abandon all of his passions in exchange for simply "trying to fit in" by partying all the time. But that had to end. I was pissed at the volume of time I had been wasting, and being pissed created the necessary friction to light a fire.

I decided I would devote myself to self-improvement. For all the years I had spent tearing down my life, I would now be dedicated to rebuilding it, and hopefully better than it was before. Even if not, I knew it would at least be different, and different was good. I immediately began consuming as much improvement stuff as possible. (Replacing alcohol, anyone?? Maybe, but it was a better option at this point.) Some of it was crap, a lot repetitive, but mostly it was useful. Today, I stand before you as someone who was able to resurrect his life and career.

At any given time, I'm usually juggling four or five jobs that I enjoy. I'm healthier than I've ever been and in the best shape of my life. No, I am not a degree-holding specialist claiming to have all the answers. I'm a Nerdy kid who fucked up a lot and learned through trial and error how to make his brain work FOR him, as opposed to AGIN him (which it has a tendency to do, as we'll see). I have determined that our abilities to effectively take action and make changes can be broken into three dimensions, which not coincidentally will make up the three sections of this book:

Mind: How you can trick your brain into working for and not agin you.

Body: A fertile mind can only be properly harvested when the machine that runs it has sufficient energy.

Time: The first two are all but useless unless you can efficiently connect the events in your life with constructive actions using Einstein's favorite dimension.

If you picked up this book, it's probably because the word "Nerdist" and its root word "Nerd" resonated with you. I think we, as Nerds, have very specific thought-processes and problem-solving approaches and so that is why I wanted to speak directly to you, to help you, and as a like-minded human, navigate some of the restrictive brain channels that might be keeping you from being where you want to be in life. And I genuinely want to help you, because our time on this spinning elemental sphere is limited, and at the very least, you deserve to be happy (most of the time). And if you DO have suppressed Nerd rage, I say to you: FINALLY a way to get even with those who stepped on your neck! DON'T wait for another social tragedy to put the fire in your belly! DON'T resort to cheap "mass-murder" tactics to exact your revenge! Success is the most satisfying and LEGAL form of revenge. It is my goal to help make you "better" than your peers. Ultimately, isn't that what we all want?

Here's what NOT to expect in this book → a ton of snarky Star Trek references (though I am happy to do that: Guinan, Sarek, the Kobayashi Maru) that feel to the reader like, "Hey, he sure is capitalizing on this Nerd thing while it's COOL!" This book is a philosophical approach to dealing with various sectors of your life that start at an emotional level: fear, anxiety, focus, physical health, time management. If you're here, it's probably because you're looking for answers. I was, too. I genuinely want you to be able to learn from my mistakes, so you can make en-

tirely NEW and innovative ones of your own and then go pass
on your knowledge to some other poor fuck!

Nerds are a community who should support each other
(though some of us tend to take such pleasure in tearing others down on message boards, but let's ignore that for now). The
sentences that make up this book are sincere, and I hope you feel
that when you read it. Despite being a loud, obnoxious comic, the
truth is I'm very private, and I'm sharing things in this book that
I don't normally share with people. It's a little scary, some of it
even embarrassing. Some of you may relate, others may write me
off as a kookbag. I just have this feeling that there are other Nerd-
types out there who suffer some of the same self-inflicted an-
guish from time to time and can't seem to get out of their own
way, so this book is for them. Even if you don't "get" every chapter, or if you emit a self-satisfying "Pfffft. Yeah, be more obvious,
why don't you??" I suspect there are a few things that will make
you reevaluate the way you drive your brain (and yes, we do drive

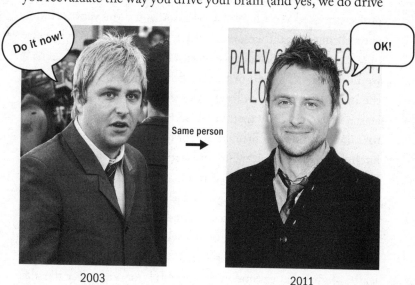

2003   2011

our brains to a much greater extent than we realize), care for your body, and manage your time. If I can do that for you, it will justify this purchase. If not, you can tweet at me with the hashtag #DoucheChimp.

Back in April 2011, I woke up one Sunday morning feeling particularly bouncy. Someone had emailed me a pic of me from 2003 in which I was decidedly blimpier. I got the "spontaneous inspiration" bug and quickly tossed up a post on Nerdist.com about how you can change your life in an instant with a simple decision. A "you can do it if you just start" kind of thing.

The response in the comment thread was moving and sweet . . . except for one. That ONE turd in the collective punchbowl at which the Web is so skilled. For every thing in the known universe, there's an opposing force to hate it. This Newtonian hatred expressed itself thusly, "What a saccharine pile of SHIT. You're not a fucking LIFE COACH, asshole. Just make with the funny and shut up." Ahhhhh, yes. That familiar feeling of disassociated Web-buse that will find you if you venture to put yourself out there in any way, which is now ALWAYS because of our concurrent digital existences. If you had infinite fingers, it would still not plug all of the acrid hate spew that leaks out of the Internet at any given time. I'm sure this book will generate at least a few more! I'm expecting it, so I'm kind of looking forward to it in a weird way. I bring it up not to whine like the proverbial bitch, but to say that it makes an excellent point: I AM NOT A LIFE COACH. I don't wish to be a motivational speaker or a self-help guru. But why do you have to be a life coach to share the spoils of your experiences? I am a dude with a Long Tail of mistakes. I have gleaned some knowledge from them. I wish to share that knowledge in hopes that other humans will have at least a slightly easier time in this world. I not only enjoy the idea of having others benefit from my flailings, I feel like it's a responsibility for me to offer them up. In short, knowledge is useless if it isn't shared.

Now that the disclaimers have been laid out, let's lower our emotional defense shields and talk about Nerds in a favorable and informative fashion!

PART ONE
MIND

YOU OWN YOUR MIND

You absolutely own your mind. It's yours. This is part of the "gift of life" thing that you get in exchange for never having asked to be born. You are the proprietor of your thoughts and feelings, and you choose how you frame the many experiences that form the campus of your personality. It's a weird and glorious moment of self-awareness the day you realize that you are the *warden* rather than the *prisoner* of your emotions. The interesting thing about our minds is that if we don't actively seize control of them, they default to autopilot. When you don't take an aggressive role in shaping your thoughts, feelings, and perceptions, you become a helpless passenger floating through the universe like a ghost ship, merely reacting to wherever it takes you. Awesomely, YOU DON'T HAVE TO GO ALONG WITH IT.

We spend so much time distracting our seemingly helpless selves while on the ghost ship when all we need is a little bit of direction and focus to ultimately assume manual control and begin piloting the ship. Nerds are preprogrammed to excel in matters of focus because our innate mental gifts allow us to do so. Are you a passenger on a ghost ship or are you the pilot? More importantly, are you a Nerd? What is a Nerd? Has it just become a diluted buzzword, rendered meaningless and devoid of soul? Possibly. But hopefully not. I mean, if I hope for anyone to give a shit about this book, that is.

The word "Nerd" is very special to me. It's been with me my whole life, and I see it in the work of every single one of my close friends, the community of wonderful humans who follow my ramblings online, and through the eyeholes of the masks of the many Cons I attend around the country. So how do I define this word?

Nerrrrrrrrrrrrrds!!!
—Ogre, *Revenge of the Nerds*

A "Nerd" is someone who homes in on a topic to an almost quantum detail, much of the time at the expense of healthy social interaction. Nerds get caught up in the minutiae because there is a tremendous and fulfilling sense of control in understanding every single detail of a thing more than any other living creature. The second important facet to a Nerd is his or her voluminous imagination and attraction to fantasy. I believe these two components of Nerds are the result of both nature AND nurture; as smarter beings, Nerds tend to obsess over mind-oriented activities and as such shy away from physical ones—like sports—and therefore suffer much social ostracizing while young. This rejection from the outside world forces them to turn inward and become more introspective and obsessive, thereby strengthening their Nerdiness.

Many times I have been told I'm not a Nerd because I don't "look like one." I think I kind of understand what this means, but it's always slightly offensive to me. Like if you tell someone you're Jewish and they say, "THAT'S funny. You don't LOOK Jewish!" Really? Offensive much? What does that look like exactly? Oftentimes, I get the Nerd denial from members of the Nerd community, which is shocking to me because if ANY group should understand the merits of exercising open-mindedness and tolerance . . .

I think what they're trying to say is that I don't seem socially awkward. Nor do I have a lightsaber attached to my hip (though for Halloween last year I was Luke Skywalker Texas Ranger and had a lightsaber awkwardly attached to my hip).

Goldie Hawn Solo and
Luke Skywalker Texas Ranger

Nor do I have to keep pushing my glasses up onto my face because of sweat slippage. These are all hacky stereotypes of Nerds. So much emphasis is placed these days on the superficial qualities of what people expect Nerds to look like and be into that the essential elements of what it means to be a Nerd are lost.

No matter the costume, Nerds obsess. We zealously deconstruct. We have a very active internal monologue (which may feel more like a dialogue sometimes). I think that so many of the things we undertake are a partial attempt to distract this monologue. We are hyper-self-aware. We have difficulty "chilling out."

A "Nerdist"—or artful Nerd—shares all of these traits, but "controls" them in a way that allows him or her to deconstruct an idea, similar to how one would in a game world, and then map out a plan so the idea can come to life. A Nerdist can also learn to turn off that internal monologue and calm the mind so that he or she can think about getting to the next level and its advanced set of rewards and challenges. And while a Nerdist will obsess and deconstruct, it's all in an effort to reach his or her goal. Interestingly, it's the Nerd's greatest weakness that is the Nerdist's greatest strength: a heightened ability to focus. Any success guru will tell you that the key to success and mastery involves focusing on a goal in a consistent manner. That's it. It's really that simple.

SIMPLE SUCCESS FORMULA!
Step 1: Choose your goal.
Step 2: Focus on it.
Step 3: That's it.

Step 1 can be challenging because even though we seem to be a culture of "GIMME GIMME GIMME," most people would be stumped if you asked them point-blank what it is that they want. It is supremely important to be able to answer this question (which I'll help you with in the next chapter), even if you change it later. I can't tell you how many times I've skipped dinner because I'm sitting in my driveway going "What sounds good??" for an hour until I give up and go to bed hungry and confused. *Know what you're specifically going after.*

Step 2 can be especially challenging not because it requires focus, but because it usually calls for shifting focus. As Nerds, we are focus MACHINES. We can steal little bits of obsession with World of Warcraft and aim it at the creation of a company or product we're passionate about. Instead of building fake civilizations, it's time we realize that we can build empires . . . IN REAL LIFE (or "IRL," in annoying cyberspeak). This is because . . . your brain is a laser.

YOUR BRAIN IS A LASER

That's right! You have LASERbrain! When stimulated properly, you can focus on something until you finish it, and in learning how to handle this laser you can better reach your goal. When I had my first PlayStation, I got sucked into an RPG called *Wild Arms*. It was in the *Final Fantasy* vein of multiplayer, quest-driven monster slaying. It was 1998. I'm not sure which month . . . all the days blended together while I was playing. I wasn't sleeping, I was KIND OF eating, and I was blowing off work stuff to stay home and play this game. When I did happen to wander outside into the world and interact with other humans, my mind was still at home, playing *Wild Arms*. This was great for my *Wild Arms* characters (Poo, Fartly, and Pretzelbread). This was bad for my career. It would take me several more years before I realized that this laser could be actively focused in better ways.

Imagine you're a young mutant, destined to become one of the X-Men. You don't know you have mutant powers, but shortly after your sixteenth birthday, you're walking home from the arcade at the mall when you notice that a girl you've always been in love with is being harassed by hooligans. In a startling burst of adrenaline, beams shoot out of your eyes and disintegrate the attackers. This is when you discover your new powers. Of course she goes out with you, but you later break up with her when you start to suspect she was just using you for your laser eyes, after which you use them to torch her Jetta.

When you were a teenager and started discovering the hobbies and interests that would define you, you probably had no problem concentrating on stuff because you were finding and learning new things. Then when you would pick those things, your focus went into hyperphase because you needed to conquer and own these passions. Recall this power and keep it tucked in the back of your think-vault as I share a story with you.

VIDEO GAMES HAVE VALUE

My father, Hall of Fame professional bowler Billy Hardwick, retired from bowling at the ripe old age of thirty-four. He then went on to open a bowling center in 1981. My parents met in 1970 when my dad was bowling at a bowling center that my mom's father owned. The point here is that I was grown in a bowling center (yes, I meant to word it that way). In the '70s, bowling centers capitalized on the addictive, quarter-munching qualities of video games when they started installing *Pong*. After all, kids whose parents were bowling in leagues needed something to do other than run around and break things. This was followed by other such phenom games like *Space Invaders*, *Asteroids*, *Pac-Man*,

Defender, and *Donkey Kong*. As we turned the corner into the neon-pop feel of the '80s, video games were moved off the bowling center concourse and into dedicated arcades. My grandfather, one Jim Facente, was a technophile. I credit all of my early Nerdist passions to his influence. He had a LaserDisc player in '79, an early Betamax (he said the quality was better than VHS—he was right), any newfangled video camera, an Atari 2600, Coleco-Vision, Intellivision . . . it was a constant stream of blinking toys. He also had the foresight to put a massive arcade in his Miami bowling hall, Palm Springs Lanes. I spent much time there. He had his arcade tech mark up a bunch of quarters with red nail polish that would then be separated and recycled for me, giving me an endless stream of arcade game play. I was a spoiled Nerd at the dawn of a digital revolution. The timing was gorgeous. When my dad opened his center, there was little question that my vote leaned heavily toward the implementation of this fair and balanced plan. Not surprisingly, I was pretty good, having spent so much time in there. My favorite (and highest scoring games) were *Robotron: 2084*, *Galaga*, *Donkey Kong Jr.*, and *Tron*.

Naturally, there was a parallel home game system marathon as well—from the earliest days of Atari's *Combat* (which came with the system) to *Adventure*, *Superman*, and *Pitfall!* Nerds, this was a golden age of gaming and I was a happily spoiled Gen X brat. It was a glorious time of discovery, when video games gave us the at-home ability to have SQUARES shoot LINES at OTHER SQUARES. Those games probably look as ridiculous to kids today as medieval barber tools look to a doctor (Atari released an emulator pack of its own games for the iPad for $15, if you want to test this theory). Still, they were no less powerful at firing a tractor beam at your brain and holding you in front of the television set indefinitely, with that archaic antenna to co-ax switchbox. How many valuable "inventing minutes" did I blow in front of those games? Who knows? I was too busy poking arrows into 8-bit dragons to care.

My game addiction continued through the years until 2004. I had an audition for some show or other that probably never saw the light of day. I bombed it. HARD. But I didn't care. I had been up all night the night before pipe-whipping pimps in *Grand Theft Auto 2*. While reading lines in the audition, all I could think about was getting back home to play more *GTA2*. This was a problem. Having recently had to quit drinking, I was on a "no addiction" addiction, so I decided to give it all up. I sold my gaming systems and all of my games on eBay for about $700 so I could focus on actual, productive work. Even today, I maintain a healthy distance from getting too involved. For this reason I have never played *WoW* (*World of Warcraft* online) because I know that I would end up donating thousands of hours to Blizzard Entertainment while paying them for the privilege.

So why are video games so addictive? First and foremost, they're an active distraction. They're constantly engaging. How the hell did kids distract themselves before video games? Probably with zoetropes and having to work in factories. Second—and I think most important—they make you feel like you're actually *doing* something. Your brain processes the tiered game achievements as REAL LIFE achievements. It's like you're accomplishing stuff! But unless you get paid to play video games, you're kind of not accomplishing stuff. Recreational gaming is fine, but once it drifts into your "I really should be doing work" life, then it's a problem (if you want to do anything substantial in the world, that is. If not, then play games until you get couch sores and ultimately have to be airlifted into a piano-sized coffin for all I care).

This is not bad news. If you've ever been obsessed with a game, you have already proven to yourself that you have the ability to focus. Rather than being all bitter about scaling back your gaming (or any obsession) and shifting to work mode, let's see if we can figure out some ways to take the training you already have and apply it to what it is you really want in life. You know how lion cubs tumble around with each other and it's all cute 'n' stuff? They're not playing for the fuck of it. They're training to destroy things later in life, and this is what we can try to do for you.

RPG YOUR LIFE

.

You probably know this, but just in case you're some kind of jock trying to infiltrate Nerd culture to dole out a monsoon of noogies when we least expect it, an RPG is a role-playing game. D&D is the most classic example. Players assume character identities and make choices in a story that ultimately affects and determines their outcome. Non-video RPGs are played with dice, and the roll of those dice represents the haphazard nature of chance that we enjoy in life. I played as recently as a few years ago in a campaign with a few other notable Nerd comedians like Brian Posehn, Blaine Capatch, and Patton Oswalt (check out his book *Zombie Spaceship Wasteland* for hilarious Nerdy goodness, btw). I miss those Sundays, crowded around Posehn's dining table, rolling twenty-sided dice and making wiener jokes, while Patton regaled us with filthy musical couplets from his drunken dwarf character, Stumphammer.

D&D is the ultimate Nerd game—where narrative meets

probability, where fantasy meets mathematics. SQUEEEEEEE!!! The other compelling component to RPGs is their reward/ achievement system. As you progress through a story, you gain things like treasure and experience points. The more points you have, the higher your level, ergo the stronger you are. It's a pretty fun distillation of life itself.

Some video games (like the *Final Fantasy* series) follow the RPG model, which is a really great model for goal achievement. You choose a path, then you have a series of smaller tasks and battles that make you stronger in order to take on harder and harder battles until you beat the final boss in the game and claim whatever ultimate prize you were seeking. It's very linear, and very applicable to your life (unfortunately without the spells and magic weapons, dammit). Mirroring this model will be very exciting to your Nerd brain and should give you the same basic charge in reality that you get from guiding your digital avatar.

DESIGN YOUR GAME

Rather than being a helpless piece of seaweed that gets knocked around by the ebb and flow of a turbulent world, you need to RIGHT NOW and IN THIS VERY MINUTE think of yourself as a GAME DESIGNER. You certainly can't control everything, but you can at least put a structure in place that tips the odds heavily in your favor.

First off, what do you want? Remember this irritating question from earlier? I tried to prepare you for it. It seems like a basic question, but even though a poor, lost Nerd might feel crappy about his life, he will nonetheless shrug his shoulders when you pose it. KNOW THIS, young slayer: You can't get things unless you know what those things are to begin with. Aha! This is where writing shit down comes into play. Go to the drugstore and buy one of those cheap graph paper notebooks. Graph paper is fun because it's gridded, and in addition to notes, it's great for making geometric wonder sketches and dot-based games, for you folks who enjoy margin doodling as much as I do. ALSO, you are literally going to make a Nerdy little map for your goals and the straight lines and 90-degree angles will be helpful. Making hierarchical lists is OK, too, but quickly sketching out a graphical representation of what you want and how to get there is much more sticky to the brain, I think. Notice how computers aren't text based anymore? Because the GUI (graphical user interface) that Apple borrowed for free from Star, the Xerox 8010 Information System, to make the Lisa in 1983 is much easier for the user and more engaging.

NERD MAPPING!!!

OK, you have your $2 graph notebook. Henceforth it shall be known as your Character Tome, just because. I like to draw on mine and slap stickers on the cover—like some kind of crazy old scientist's journal. Did you figure out what you want yet? If not, start making lists of things you want and things you'd like to do. If your brain feels soupy, it may be because you've been carrying around too much crap in it so it's important to pull that out onto the paper and into the physical world. (If you're a fan of David Allen's GTD routine, this will be familiar.) Once you have a list of things you want—some might be short-term goals and others long term—order them by level of difficulty, that is, how hard you think it will be to acquire them. Then draw a line around one row of cells from the left to right X axes on the graph paper. Every few cells, make a vertical notch and over each of the notches write the things you want to achieve in order of difficulty from easiest to hardest. Art time! Over those words, draw little representations of each thing. It's fun, and pictures will resonate more with your molecules than words. This will be your overall game map. You can always adjust the goal points later, but this will give you a good place to start. Over the whole thing write a time frame. It can be any amount of time, but putting yourself on the clock to achieve this series of goals is the key. (See examples at NerdistWay.com)

Now, take each individual goal that you notched and make the same long, horizontal single-cell rectangle. These long boxes will become your Progress Bars. Under each goal-related Progress Bar, write as many steps as you can think of that will move you toward this goal, no matter how small. As you complete each one of these steps, color in your Progress Bar a little bit more until it's full, which would indicate the completion of your goal! As you complete each goal, you will begin to fill in the cells on your OVERALL Progress Bar that you made first. It sounds screwy but it makes sense if you see it in action, so go to Nerdist Way.com for a demonstration of this madness.

CHARACTER PAGE

When you play any of the pen-and-paper RPGs, the very first thing you have to do is "roll your character," which means throwing a bunch of dice to determine how attractive, smart, or smelly your character is. Then you write all of that down on a template so you have a quick character reference. I think this is PERFECT for life. You're going to make a Character Page where you are the character. First of all, you won't have to roll any dice. You'll only have to fill in a few values after an honest assessment of your traits. While we are all very complex beings, it is very freeing to condense yourself into a handful of attributes that will give you not only a much better sense of who you are, but also a convenient reference point to help inform your decision making. Douche bags are like robots: They lack self-awareness. YOU are a Nerd. There is an excellent chance that self-awareness is one of your defining qualities. As such, pulling a few of your traits into the physical world and assigning values to them will help simplify things a bit by enlightening you with regard to yourself.

On the top left corner of the first page of your open graph notebook, write your name (or whatever snazzy alias you want your inner self to be called). I once drew myself as a wizard and called him Blavidane, a flip-flopped name of gravitas stunt magician and fellow attention-slut David Blaine. If you really want an über-Nerd fantasy-sounding name but can't think of one, Wizards of the Coast (owners of the D&D franchise) has a great name generator at nerdi.st/NameGenerator. I went on just now and got the name Varolin Quifflock. I know, you're jealous. Or horny.

Underneath that, write out these six attributes next to a cell where you will fill in a value from 1 to 5:

Intelligence: Pretty self-explanatory, don't you think, Genius Bar?

Charisma: How magnetic or influential are you over other life-forms?

Strength: Can you do a sit-up? What kind of shape are you in?

Wisdom: Different from intelligence; you may be smart, but do you make healthy decisions?

Will: Can you commit to things even when you don't feel like doing them?

Confidence: Are you comfortable in your skin? Are your decisions accompanied by conviction?

Since you will probably be the only person who sees this (that may be best, anyway), be honest in your assessment of yourself. The cool thing about these numbers is that they are not set for life. As you gain experience points through making choices in your life and learning from your successes and mistakes, you might feel periodically inclined to adjust these numbers. Seeing a numerical value on your Will, por esample, may very well encourage you to commit to tasks better if only for the pure joy of being able to raise that number a point.

CHOOSE YOUR ALIGNMENT

According to part-time truth seeker Wikipedia, "Alignment is a categorisation [sic] of the moral and ethical perspective of the player characters." In other words, what do you stand for? Knowing which way your moral wiener points can be very helpful when faced with tough decisions.

The official position on alignment* comes from Wizards of the Coast (Wizards.com):

Alignment is central to a D&D character's personality. D&D uses two measures to determine a specific character's ethical and moral attitudes and behavior.

---

* Official guideline assist from the D&D alignment wiki on Wikipedia; Examples of each came from *Complete Scoundrel: A Player's Guide to Trickery and Ingenuity*. If none of this makes sense to you or your eyes have started bleeding in defiance, you can go to nerdi.st/AlignmentTest on Wizards.com to take a quick alignment test to determine where you fall. S'fun!

The moral axis has three positions: good, neutral, and evil. Good characters generally care about the welfare of others. Neutral people generally care about their own welfare. Evil people generally seek to harm the others' welfare.

The ethical axis has three positions as well: lawful, neutral, and chaotic. Lawful people generally follow the social rules as they understand them. Neutral people follow those rules [they] find convenient or obviously necessary. And chaotic people seek to upset the social order and either institute change, or simply create anarchy.

ALIGNMENTS

LAWFUL GOOD, "CRUSADER"

The Boy Scout! Lawful Good people are saintly do-gooders who tend to get boners for honor and duty to a higher authority. EXAMPLES: Batman, Dick Tracy, and Indiana Jones.

NEUTRAL GOOD, "BENEFACTOR"

Whereas Lawfuls follow a third-party code, Neutrals are bound by their own conscience. They will act altruistically, whether or not their actions are technically "legal." EXAMPLES: Zorro and Spider-Man. I'd pitch The Doctor in this pile, but some Nerds would shout that he's more the next one down, Chaotic Good.

CHAOTIC GOOD, "REBEL"

My personal favorite alignment, Chaotic Good, is synonymous with "the lovable rebel." The characters are drawn toward a greater good, but have little care for any political authority unless it gibes with their own agenda. In fact, they may tend to buck authority just because they don't like the idea of being under someone's thumb. They are not above doing bad stuff and getting their hands dirty if it serves that good in the end. And oh yeah . . . LADIES LOVE THESE GUYS (and vicey versey). EXAMPLES: Starbuck from *Battlestar Galactica*, Malcolm Reynolds from *Firefly*, and Robin Hood. My addition: Dexter Morgan.

LAWFUL NEUTRAL, "SOLDIER"

Are you dogmatic? Do you enjoy an abdicratic existence where you do everything you're told in an effort to never question your authority of choice? There's no real allegiance to a greater good or evil, just tradition and orders. EXAMPLES: James Bond, Odysseus, and Kiefer Sutherland's mush-mouthed marine in *A Few Good Men*.

NEUTRAL, "UNDECIDED"

Welcome to On-the-Fence-Berg. If you're Neutral, there isn't any other alignment that really suits you. You also might be an animal, as animals do not have the burden of moral and ethical concerns. If you really feel like this one is you in a nutshell, then fine, but I don't recommend it. It's too vague, IMHO. EXAMPLES: full-time stoners or a chicken running around your yard.

CHAOTIC NEUTRAL, "FREE SPIRIT"

ANARCHY!!! If all you give a crap about is yourself and your own wants and needs without regard for anyone or anything, this is you. You're pretty much free to do whatever you want, and you will probably undermine authority just for the sake of undermining authority. EXAMPLES: Captain Jack Sparrow, Al Swearengen from *Deadwood*, and Snake Plissken.

LAWFUL EVIL, "DOMINATOR"

If you ever rub your hands together diabolically while uttering a crescendoing "mwua-ha-HA-HA!!!!" then you are Lawful Evil.

Isn't it nice to FINALLY have a name for it? You do follow a code of conduct, or a leader, and while you wouldn't go out of your way to crush someone, you would take great pleasure in leveling anyone or anything that gets in your way. EXAMPLES: Boba Fett and Magneto.

NEUTRAL EVIL, "MALEFACTOR"

These guys are not needlessly destructive, but they also don't follow any higher code. They are guided by their own desires and will only pledge allegiance to those who will help them get what they want, and then turn on them later if it suits them. EXAMPLES: General Zod and Sawyer of the early seasons of *Lost*. And why not add Megatron just cuz?

CHAOTIC EVIL, "DESTROYER"

Not only are these jerks guided only by their own desires, but those desires are almost always cruel and awful. Demons, monsters, most serial killers ('cept Dexter). They enjoy the torture and suffering of others. Best to stay away from this lot. EXAMPLES: Carl Denham from *King Kong*, Riddick from *Pitch Black*, Darth Maul, and Sauron from *The Lord of the Rings*.

Why the hell would you bother with all of this? Well, because it's fun. MORE IMPORTANTLY, few people ever stop to reflect on how they approach the world. They just react without really thinking about it (how's that ghost ship working for ya?). *The idea here is for you to use this exercise to start to figure out who you are.* Having a stronger yet compact sense of how you are aligned with the world will help inform your goal setting and decision making. RELATED STORY ALERT! I took four years of Latin in high school. "But that's a DEAD language! Why toil in such linguistic necrophilia??" Besides the fact that English (despite being a Germanic language) has more than half of its roots in Latin, it creates an understanding of language STRUCTURE that you don't really get with your native language. I had never heard of "pluperfect tense," "subjunctive mood" and "passive voice." They were terms I had always employed but never recognized. You just intuitively speak your first language without paying much attention to WHY you make the choices you do because you mainly learn to communicate through social interaction. When people talk at you, they rarely say, "Eat your vegetables! That's in the imperative voice!" so you never think about it.

By identifying yourself as a character and dissecting your why's and points of view, you gain a bit more of this same structural clarity. It will give you more control with regard to picking between choices A and B, provide you with emotional shortcuts to keep you from agonizing over low-level problem solving, and even lay down a foundation for being able to manipulate yourself to accomplish things, which you will have to do from time to time.

Now . . . *we need weapons*!

INVENTORY OF WEAPONS

Now that you know how you react to life, let's outfit you with some weaponry! While you may not have access to maces, morning stars, and broadswords, you have skill sets. These will be your weapons. Write down everything you are fairly capable of doing on a sheet of paper. Next to each skill, rate your proficiency from 1 to 5, with 1 being weak and 5 being strong. (This is a VERY loose interpretation of how D&D works, so don't yell at me in all caps about how this isn't textbook D&D. I know.) When you're done you might have something that looks like this:

Illustration +5
HTML +3
WordPress +4
Photoshop +5
Video editing +3
Crocheting +5
Negotiating +1
Communication +2

You will probably have more than this, but this will give you a basic grid of what you're good at, and what you might be interested in but need to work on. It also might inform you as to the types of work you are able to pursue. In this configuration you will see that you could probably launch a craft website with an emphasis on creating graphical yarn art. After all, you have +5 Hooks of Dexterity in your arsenal. Remember, as you improve in certain areas, you get to adjust these numbers. As silly as it sounds, it is oddly gratifying.

EXPERIENCE POINTS!

In RPGs your character gains strength by earning XP (experience points), which I find to be an excellent concept. The idea of goal achievement is really about breaking larger goals into smaller, bite-size goals that collectively draw you toward the larger one. Nerds are collectors: Comics, games, figures, and vintage items are examples. We are masters at acquiring items that revolve around a central theme. We also enjoy collecting points. Doesn't matter for what. Points are cool. When the Wii first came out, I actually photographed the screen for my first 300 in Wii Bowling (#humblebrag). Goal attainment through numerical rewards is a dynamic achievement system, and if you have to slightly trick your brain into acquiring more points with the result of getting shit done, I would say, "INITIATE BRAIN TRICKERY PROTOCOL."

MonkeySushi (monkeysushi.net) gives the following function used by D&D for leveling up:

$$\text{XP required for next level} = 1000 \times [\text{level} + C\,(\text{level}, 2)]$$
$$\text{where } C \text{ is the combinatoric function}$$

This is likely to upset you, so let's just simplify the formula. First, assign numerical values to your goals: 5 points for easy tasks, 10 points for medium difficulty, 25 for heavy lifting, and 100 points for completing big projects. At the end of the day or week (however frequently you like), add up your points and write them down on the Experience Page of your Character Tome. You start at Level 1, so every time you hit 100 points, level up. As your goal completions accumulate, in no time at all you could be a 12th Level Graphic Designer, or a 15th Level Webmaster. As you become more successful, those 100 pointers will get more challenging as you're afforded the opportunity to take on bigger and more complex projects. If you have an iPhone, pick up Rex Box and Super Mono Studios' *Epic Win* app (rexbox.co.uk/epic win), which does pretty much the same thing but with kick-ass animations and sound effects.

Finally, draw your character! (This was a requirement in my grade school campaigns.) Make it your Image Ideal or your Ironic Image Ideal (my Xbox avatar is an Indian guy with a face mole and a leather vest). Do you have armor? Weapons? Wings? Are you human even? Make an artistic representation of who you want to be. This will live on your Character Page, which should also be the first page of your Character Tome. Are you a crappy illustrator? No worries! Make a Photoshop-style mashup of your avatar or simply print out a pic you like and tape it into your Character Tome. The idea is that you have a visual representation to remind you of your path whenever you start getting a case of the "doubties."

Why would I encourage you to do all of this ridiculous business? Because, sweet Nerdling, I want to get you engaged in achieving your goals. Maybe it's launching your passion career or maybe it's more about finding a creative outlet. Writing, drawing, and adding values to your goals will force you to (a) figure out what you WANT, (b) figure out who YOU are, and (c) establish an achievement/reward structure that will push you in the direction of accomplishing stuff. It's also fun. Is "fun" a good enough reason to do stuff sometimes? I think so.

As you go through the rest of the book, you will see the heading "Charactercize." It's a dumb word I thought of to mean "Here is a question or exercise for you to answer or do in your Character Tome."

SEIZE YOUR INNER MONOLOGUE

If things aren't going the way you want them to, there's a very simple answer: You suck. You suck and everything you try to do ends up in a failure pile. If you regularly made cakes, their composition would somehow turn into shit with maggot jimmies by the time they came out of the oven. Sure, you can try to do good things to get ahead, but the universe is conspiring against you. OF COURSE that thing you wanted didn't work out. Why would it? Why would ANYTHING, for that matter? It's YOU we're talking about!!!

Now that you see this written down you might understand how ridiculous it is the next time you go to this place mentally. One of the biggest themes of this book (and hopefully your life) is this: *Go easy on yourself*. External forces trying to attack you in this world can be difficult enough. Don't add to them by attacking yourself. Not only will you get that "never clean" feeling, but you'll sabotage all of the good things that you are working for and absolutely deserve.

WHY THINGS DON'T GO YOUR WAY

If you enjoy philosophy or physics, then you must know that perspective is everything. Events are inherently valueless. WE assign values *to* them. How you perceive something gives it its value. Two people can perceive the same thing in completely opposite ways, and both would seem valid for each person (look up "parallax" just for fun). It is through this lens that you begin to realize the power you have to shape your reality. What is reality? It's merely a string of perceptions that you navigate. Control your perceptions and you control your reality. Why, if you were a solipsist, you would actually think that NOTHING outside your own perspective actually exists. That would mean that from my point of view, you are an extension of my psyche reading my book, and from yours, I wrote this in your mind. See why philosophy is so much fun? OK, fuck solipsism.

It is very likely that when things don't pan out the way you intended, you kick the shit out of yourself. You reason that this is yet another in a long chain of events that are part of a master plan on the part of the Universe to conspire with the Elements against you. This is naturally a pile of Orc shit. No one is conspiring against you. This isn't just "how it is" for you. Nerds, because they tend to tune in to their inner monologue more than regular folks, many times will assume the most selfish point of view. To think that the Universe (a) is sentient and (b) would focus all or even part of its energy to ensure your unhappiness is laughable and more than a little self-centered. But it's not all the Nerd's fault. It's human nature to attach reasoning to events in an attempt to understand an otherwise reasonless world, no matter how ridiculous. (AHEMreligionAHEM COUGHthough notjudgingyouifyouarereligiousCOUGH.) For people who normally operate from pragmatic and logical places, it is surprisingly superstitious.

CHARACTERCIZE

 What are some reasons you think things aren't working out for you?

 Write them in your Character Tome so you can see how ridiculous they are.

 Then write "BULLSHIT" with an arrow pointing to them. Add cartoon flies hovering over for effect.

RECALL THAT SELF-AWARENESS

It is important to peel back your brain layers to see if there's something that motivates you to think this way. You may feel on a subconscious level that you don't deserve good things in life, but you're just making that up without realizing it. My father, one of the greatest professional bowlers of all time (don't mean to brag, ladies), fell into such a spiral of despair in his thirties because of some horrible happenstance—namely the deaths of two sons—that he developed the following association: When good things happen, bad things happen shortly after. It was because of this destructive yet false polarity that he lost his passion for the game at which he was so good and retired at thirty-four.

Here's a related joke: Two Irish Catholics are on a cliff watching the sunset. As the sky spills a palette of reds and oranges around the fiery orb, they quickly realize that it is absolutely the most beautiful sunset they or possibly anyone has ever seen. They stare at it in awe for several moments until one finally turns to the other and says, "Oh, we're gonna pay for this one!" Look, good things happen and bad things happen. They're usually not connected in some kind of unholy marriage of crap. It's a fallacy but one that is fairly common. So what is it? It's a form of self-sabotage. It could stem from an erroneous association, like in my father's case, or maybe its roots go back generations. As someone who attended an all-boys Catholic school, I love the Irish Catholic reference in the aforementioned joke because Catholicism operates heavily on an economy of guilt. Jews know this, too. I'm sure fifteen hundred years ago, when religion and politics and science were all the same thing, the people in power realized that it was better to keep the masses from striving for greatness and upsetting that balance of power, so they taught them that aiming too high would anger the Lord. "Who would ever want to anger the wizard that created us? We'd better keep our heads low and stay evenly within the median. In fact, I should probably flagellate myself for even entertaining any ideas of getting ahead." [whipping sounds] This is still ingrained in our emotional DNA. But it's foolish, and hopefully the mere fact that you are aware of it will help dissipate its evil grasp on your soul.

Think about it: Why don't you deserve good things in life? Why shouldn't you have everything you want? Material wealth, for example, is a man-made concept. If you were to step back to the edge of the solar system, next to poor, downgraded Pluto, you would quickly see that it has no real positive or negative value in the universe. If you make shit-tons of money, just as one example, the Universe doesn't really care one way or the other. And don't think that I'm saying money is everything. It isn't, if you don't care about it. Do you want spiritual wealth? GREAT. Familial wealth? START MAKIN' BABIES! You need to determine whatever it is that's important to you before you can start tackling why you aren't getting it.

Maybe there's another possibility as to why things aren't going your way: You're a control freak. If you put yourself and your work out there even a little in this world, chances are that you're going to get rejected a percentage of the time. Those are just the odds. One way to look at it is that if you're not getting rejected a bunch, you may not be trying to innovate. When we get rejected it feels like the rug gets ripped out from underneath us, or like we're in an earthquake—we feel helpless and out of control. Naturally, it would be easy to assume that we're going to fail, so that we don't have to feel helpless. I bet you think: "At least I feel like I have control if I assume things are going to turn out shitty, so why fuckin' bother?" We might even start going there merely because it's a familiar, comfortable place, similar to how someone might stay in an abusive relationship.

Try playing chess with an ape. He opens with the classic e2-e4 but you choose to use the Pirc Defense. He hadn't counted on this. In a fit of rage, he knocks over the board and then bites your genitals. When you jump to the "failure place" out of frustration, you are the ape in that scenario. It'll take a good bit of effort in the beginning, but try to avoid assuming the worst-case scenario just to protect your feelings. Becoming stagnant because you're the Mayor of WhyBotherTon can't teach you anything. It's a path to nowhere. At least with rejection and failure, you can learn something for next time. If you can believe you deserve good things and cultivate this skill of "putting yourself out there no matter what," you will be ahead of 98 percent of the humans on this eroding rock.

YOUR INTERNAL CHARLIE ROSE

Ask. Good. Questions. This may be the single most important thing you can do in your life. Instead of screaming "WTF???" every time something lame happens, ask more effective questions of yourself. "Why do I suck?" is useless. Your brain will answer you with something like, "Because you masturbated in a church that one time," because it is wired to give you an answer no matter what. Make it work FOR you. You need to become a regular fucking Charlie Rose with your own mind. Would you agree that Rose is one of the most superb interviewers of our time? (Just say yes.) It's largely because he's thoughtful and asks great questions. You can do this with yourself. Envision a round table against a black backdrop with you on one side and your failure on the other. Now interview it. "What REALLY went wrong? How could I have made this better? Was the hitch an unforeseeable one? What can I learn from this to improve future iterations?" Stare your failure in the face and grill it. Don't blink. Charlie never blinks.

CHARACTERCIZE

 What are some recent "failures" in your life?

 What are some lessons you can pull from them?

 Is Charlie Rose a cyborg?

BOMBING = GOOD

Bombing in front of a large group of strangers is probably the biggest nonlethal fear scenario humans have as a species. As a comic, I have been there and, truthfully, it doesn't feel amazing. Bombing is probably the most succinct representation for failure there is. You try something → you immediately know it doesn't work → you get negative feedback → you feel awful. The BEST part is, you get to look into the disappointed faces of your audience and really *feel* their indifference to your work! [fistpump]

If you can get through bombing in life, many other things become breezy. If you have the "defective comic gene," as I call it, you will still, for some crazy reason, get up and try it all again the next night. This may be because once you have bombed, you realize that (1) it's not as bad as you thought it would be, (2) you live through it, and (3) you can figure out how to fix it for next time. In fact, bombing is ESSENTIAL in comedy. It keeps you fresh and on your toes. If you killed with the same jokes night after night and never attempted to grow as a performer, you'd get bored, the jokes would get stale, and people would stop coming to see you.

I use stand-up as an example because whatever creative endeavor you're pursuing, you're not going to bomb any worse than a comedian. With comedy, building a bulletproof set is all about tweaking on the fly and learning from your mistakes. The flip side is that when something you're making isn't going over, you have the opportunity to make it better. It forces your brain into a space of "OK! Let's roll up our sleeves and make this shit work." Usually, you come up with WAY better stuff than you had the first time. As far as that "dirty on the inside" feeling you get after a bad show—where you wish you could take some Comet and a scrub brush to your soul—it goes away! AND it builds character.

No human ever became interesting by not failing. The more you fail and recover and improve, the better you are as a person. Ever meet someone who's ALWAYS had EVERYTHING work out for them with ZERO struggle? They usually have the depth of a puddle. Or they don't exist.

Besides, just because you bomb doesn't necessarily mean you were wrong. Sometimes the chemistry of a situation didn't create the right timing. With stand-up, I don't write jokes to pander to the audience. I also don't just write inside jokes I know the audience won't get because "I'm gonna do whatever I'm gonna do and SCREW everybody else, MAN!" I think it's about forming a relationship. And in a relationship, there's a give-and-take. Sometimes relationships just don't work no matter how much we want them to. Don't purposely alienate people with your craft, but also don't lose yourself trying to please everybody. Remember, when you try to talk to everyone, you're actually talking to NO ONE.

TWELVE ORBITING SATELLITES

I believe we all have a certain number of images that circle our brain at all times and that give us a general sense of who we think we are. For me that number seems to be twelve. You might have more or less, which I don't know because I don't live in your head. (Unless you're a solipsist.) Imagine your brain is a planet, and there are a bunch of satellites projecting these emotional images. I think this is because one image alone wouldn't convincingly define us, so we create a sampling to weigh against one another to evoke a single, consistent self-image.

I'm sure it feels like we're not in control of these satellites and that they just autonomously fire off things we're supposed to believe, but that just isn't true. We unconsciously give control to these internal machines because controlling them takes some energy and work. Try something: Look up from this book for a second and check in with yourself. Ask "Who am I?" You might feel a flash of events that try to satisfy this query. How did it make you feel? Do you agree with it? (I did this just now and got an image of myself in a straitjacket, cackling wildly while sinking into a volcano with pages of my unfinished book flash-popping into ash midair. I think my brain is telling me I'm crazy for trying to finish a book in a Starbucks on successive hour-long breaks from my other job.) Would you like it to be something different? It can. Isolate one of those images, focus on it, and replace it with whatever you want. Even if it's something that never happened. Now put this image into the rotation and let it go. I removed the volcano image and shoved in one in which I'm hovering above a body of water, as an elemental whirlwind forms to put a finished manuscript in my hands. A beam of light strikes my chest, Nature is singing, and I'm fairly certain a cluster of naiads just anointed my nipples. I know. I'm weird. But I can't deny that it changes the emotional value of what I was feeling before. If you do it right, and really visualize it, you should feel it, maybe even tingling, in the top of your head. You've just altered the Matrix. Congratulations, Neo!

CHARACTERCIZE

 Describe some of your images.

 Identify the negative ones.

 Try replacing them with positive ones (or even ridiculous ones).

IGNORE YOUR BRAIN

Guess what, braingineers?? I'm about to upend your world with one li'l sentence. A simple mantra that has guided me through the darkest whispers of autocerebral asphyxiation: *YOU DON'T HAVE TO BELIEVE EVERYTHING YOU THINK.* I know, RIGHT?? If you are having trouble uploading positive images to your ego satellites, here is a great tactic: Ignore your fucking brain altogether. It rarely occurs to anyone that you don't have to listen to your brain or do what it says. Your brain doesn't mean to lead you in bad directions! It really has what it perceives to be your best interests at heart. It's just that, unless properly trained, it usually only takes into account your short-term happiness because it just wants you to feel good in the immediate moment. "Get drunk in the morning!" "Eat fifty Chocodiles!" "Instead of working, you could masturbate!" These are all examples of things that will only bring you temporary happiness in that moment, but could have negative long-term effects. You can simply say to yourself, "I hear what you're saying, brain, but I choose to ignore you." If your brain rages beyond that, you can actually diffuse it by acknowledging its request and explaining in detail why it could be devastating were you to honor it.

A comedy theater I've had the extreme pleasure of performing at for the last several years is the UCB (Upright Citizens Brigade) in New York and L.A. Founders Matt Besser, Matt Walsh, Ian Roberts, and Amy Poehler were students of Improv Olympic in Chicago and trained by improv legend Del Close himself. In addition to showcasing some of the best performers in comedy, the UCB also has improv training classes. If you buy a sticker, T-shirt, or sweatshirt from the UCB, it's likely to have the following imperative phrase on it: "Don't Think." Of course, there are many, many more rules to good improv, but the basic philosophy is solid. Don't let your brain get in your way and disrupt your flow.

In 2008, Rob Zombie called me (lemme just pick up that name I dropped) and asked if my Nerdy musical comedy band Hard 'n Phirm (i.e., Chris Hardwick and Mike Phirman) would be interested in doing the theme song to an animated film he was making, *The Haunted World of El Superbeasto*, which was based on his comic book of the same name. "Of course, Rob Zombie!" I said. After we turned it in, Rob called back and said, "Would you want to just go ahead and do all of the songs so there's a consistent comedic tone to the music? Only thing is, we're in the process of mixing sound so we'd need them all, well, now . . ." "Uh . . . sure, Rob. We can . . . do that . . . NO PROBLEM." [nervous chuckle, pee trickle exits body]

So we did it. In five days. The process went like this: Get the scene in the morning that needed a song, write it, record it, send it back. From start to finish, each song took about six hours. It was like a goddamn comedy music boot camp. And it was AWESOME. It was easily one of the most valuable writing experiences of my life. We didn't have time to second-guess. We didn't have time to procrastinate with doubts. And you know what? I can't say we would have been any happier with the results had we labored and pulled our hair out over it. Granted, Rob didn't love every single one of them. We turned in one song called "Velvet Von Black's Theme" that he HATED. I got the call at 8:00 a.m. "Hey, yeah, that's not really directionally where I wanted to go with that." Despite his image, Rob did not pull our still-beating hearts out of our rib cages while slurping out the blood to a cackling demonic incantation. He's a kind and thoughtful dude. Because we had zero time to beat ourselves up about it, we took a completely different pass, which ended up becoming his favorite track of the lot.

Aside from trying to tell you what your limitations are, your brain will also try to run emotion programs to get you to react to things spontaneously. As cool as it would be, however, YOU ARE NOT A ROBOT, and you can choose not to run these programs. Here's another example! As a cable and new media "star," I get a lot of emails/tweets/comments from people about various things. Sometimes it's to tell me I suck or it's an aggressive query as to why I would do something I did. One time the E! channel aired an episode of my show *Web Soup* in place of an episode of the original *The Soup*. Sacrilege, I know. The email went something like this:

> Hey asshole. The next time you decide to run your shitty show instead of *The Soup*, can you please let my fucking DVR know so I don't have to look at your stupid face???

There were several things that made me laugh about this. Number one, any email that starts with the salutation "Hey asshole" is going to be gold. Second, I appreciate the fact that this gentleman thinks I have enough power at NBC Universal to inform programming decisions. Third, he seems to think I'm a DVR Whisperer who can talk to machinery. My first impulse was to invite him to eat a dick salad with fuck-off dressing. But then I imagined what his day might have been like. He probably worked hard at a crappy job he hates, and one can only assume that the fact that he clearly has acid for blood and spiders where his heart should be would scare off any possibility for human companionship. *The Soup* is his weekly ritual that got interrupted by my snarky mug. OF COURSE he'd be pissed and looking for someone to unleash his venom at. He either just had a bad day or is generally unhappy. Happy people simply don't go into slaughter mode over non-life-threatening situations. Bearing that in mind, I took this approach:

> Dude, I hear you. And I understand. I wouldn't want to watch me instead of Joel McHale either. Sorry it happened, but I'm sure it was just a one-time thing.
>
> Manhugs,
> Chris

What I got back was a sheepish response:

> Man, I'm sorry I went off like that. Thanks for getting back to me. I'll give your show a shot. Hope we're cool.

The trick was that he reacted emotionally in the moment—like your brain tends to—but once he felt he was being heard and that he was being taken seriously, he backed down. This is how it can work with your brain. When it angrily demands that you do something that you know isn't good for you, you can literally say to yourself, "I hear you. I get what you're saying. But what you're asking of me will cause more damage for [this, this, and this reason], and I'm not going to do it." I have actually felt my rage drain out of my head, like a snake retreating into its hole. The first time you do this, I promise you will feel a sense of lightness and liberation. Strength isn't about the attack. True strength is often the ability to NOT follow every impulse. "Act" don't "react." Make sensible choices rather than letting your emotions fling you around like a rodeo lariat.

CHARACTERCIZE

 What are your emotional triggers?

 What are some things your brain tells you to do that you know are damaging?

 What's a good response to sidestep those orders?

RAGE-MUNICATION

NEVER EMAIL, TEXT, TWEET or CALL people while experiencing negative emotions! These are almost ALWAYS the communications you wish you could ⌘-Z (CTRL-Z for PC-tizens). When you find your internal juices boiling up to your neck and face, this is exactly the time NOT to type an email. When your anger flares up, your stupid takes over. The amygdalae, reptilian brain structures that regulate emotion (which I also call "lizard almonds" because of their function and shape), take over your higher brain functions. You aren't making awesome choices at this point because you are in animal defense mechanism mode. If you give into it, you are likely to look around after you regain composure to see a trail of broken objects and friendships that you will vigorously begin scrambling to tape back together while shouting, "Lizard almonds, WHAT HAVE YOU DONE???" My advice is immediately walk away. Change your environment. Go in another room, walk around the block. Think of it as a chemical tide that needs a few minutes to ebb back down to its dank lair at the base of your brain. If you need to, say something to yourself like, "Oh, lizard almonds! Won't you EVER learn?! Now, back to the cave with you, or I'll make you stare at yawning kitty videos for a half hour!" This is ridiculous, but may actually pull you out of your anger long enough to realize it.

BREAKING THROUGH "THE WALL"

Everything's going GREAT! Your workflow is pouring out of your fingers and orifices with the fluidity of the waterfall in the opening credits of *Fantasy Island*. You're moving ever swifter toward the completion of your goal and then, quite suddenly, ka-SMASH! Seemingly out of nowhere a wall appears. You hit it, face first, and fall backward, your eyes filling with salty pools and your nose flooding with the scent of pain. You're stuck. The previously open field of creativity has now turned into a labyrinth of inactivity. If you could just punch through that wall! But each step toward it becomes increasingly more labored, like the running-through-tar feeling you get in a dream.

Every creative person everywhere knows "The Wall." It's that mental roadblock that seizes up your thoughts and convinces you that you have absolutely nothing to contribute. There are four suggestions I have to Hulk-smash through this.

1. Create anyway. You may *think* you have nothing to express, but you may be wrong. The problem is you're "thinking" about it too much. If you're a writer, for example, just start spewing words onto the page. It doesn't matter if they're sucky or even related to your current project. You have to get the gears turning to unstick them. Kinda like running a car every so often so the battery doesn't die.

None of the work we did on *The Haunted World of El Superbeasto* or since then would have been possible had we let our brains get in the way. While writing lyrics and throwing music for *Superbeasto*, we'd say, "This is good for now. We can always change it later!" Remember, your first draft doesn't have to be your FINAL draft. And if you're not crazy about something you're laying down, just call it a placeholder until you get a better idea, which you will have once all of the basic elements are in place. It was more important to get material down and in place rather than kill it by debating with ourselves before we even tried to make anything at all. I recommend NEVER prejudging your work before you start, because you NEVER WILL. Get it down. Start the process.

2. Write something hacky. My friend and manager Alex was a wunderkind who started managing bands when he was in college. He said one trick that some of these bands had to get through The Wall was to abandon all judgment and write the absolute hackiest song they could think of. More often than not, the song didn't turn out hacky. They had filters and a way of expressing their work such that the end result was usually pretty cool. All they had to do was stop thinking that inspiration had to come from some ethereal plane and get to work.

3. Trust yourself and the work. When Phirm and I are making songs, we put in the basic stuff and say this hippie thing to ourselves: "The song will tell us what it needs." The work itself takes on a personality of its own and it will tell you what it needs to be finished—a harmony here, a melodica accent there (ALWAYS recommended), lose the second chorus, etc. While writing this book, I didn't know EXACTLY what I was going to say all at once. I wrote a little each day, and trusted that, tomorrow, or in a week, I'd have other—or even better—stuff to say. Creating anything is a cumulative process and builds on the foundations of the stuff that comes before it. Many times you won't know what that is until you're well under way. Don't worry about what color you want the roof to be before you even put up the walls, friend!

4. Change your environment. Your creative work is an expression of your environment. You are a filter that processes data in a certain way and sometimes, like *Short Circuit*'s Number 5, you NEED. INPUT. You can either accomplish this by reading a totally random book to kick-start new thoughts or simply by changing your environment temporarily. I wrote this book in hotels, on planes, at home, in other people's office buildings. If I was writing at the G4 compound in Los Angeles and I hit The Wall (usually ninety minutes in), I would pack up my laptop and go across the street to Starbucks. That location shift was usually enough to get me going again. When I got tired there, I'd go somewhere else.

The key to the invisible door in The Wall is not to think of NOW as your only opportunity. Give yourself the freedom to take multiple passes at things. (BONUS: Working this way is FAR less stressful.) Ignore your brain when it tells you you'll never get something done. Trust yourself. You'll make it work.

YOU ARE THE WARDEN

As previously stated, the brain doesn't just tell you to do things; it also has a nasty habit of telling you what you CAN'T do—whether or not it's true. As you go through life you gather self-imposed limits here and there until one day you're unknowingly trapped in a prison of bullshit limitations. But the truth is, it's a holographic prison manufactured by your mind in a clumsy attempt to protect you from potential pain. Fortunately, you can walk through the fake walls anytime you want. *Be the warden, not the prisoner.*

You have the power to give those limitations zero credence and do what you want to do anyway. This may piss your brain off at first because it does not like being ignored, but after boiling a few rabbits in your mental kitchen, eventually it will bend to your Will. It's like the ghost from that movie that can only haunt people when they give it attention, and when they do, it tries to touch their boobs. You know that one movie? No? Me neither. I think I made that up. Hang on [calling out of room]: "Denise! Get my agent Morty on the phone! I gotta pitch him a supernatural erotic thriller!" [returning to chapter] In any case, push past the barrier and you will hop right back on track. Be the boss of your brain! It works for YOU, dammit!

CHARACTERCIZE

 Come up with the dumbest, hackiest thing you can think of. (And don't say, "Like your book?! Heh-heh." I got my eye on you, Trolls!)

 How can you start tweaking it to make it your own?

 Is there a project you've been putting off because of prejudgment? What is it?

 What are some limitations you've imposed on yourself? Is it possible they're not true?

CHOO-CHOO-CHOOOOOSING

I played tournament chess from fifth grade through high school. Before school, during lunch, and after school, I was on the other side of a chessboard from some other Nerd. Then many weekends there would be chess tournaments. (Ladies will be sexually aroused to know that I was the Memphis City Junior High Chess Champion of 1984.) What happens when you play THAT much chess (at least for me) was that I inadvertently taught myself to look for EVERY POSSIBLE CHOICE ALWAYS. Playing out ten moves ahead with each significant piece on a chessboard is GREAT for winning those sex-ensuring chess trophies, but it's a bit of a hindrance in life. It made it somewhat difficult for me to make decisions about things, because I was (and still am sometimes) constantly in the mode of playing out scenarios and weighing options ad infinitum.

If you're lucky, half of your decisions in life will be black or white: It's clear that one choice is superior to the other. The truth is, most choices are gray—there are some great points and some crappy downsides to every angle. This leads to a lot of things not getting done for fear of making an inferior decision. Once, I wouldn't refresh my Web site design for MONTHS because I couldn't decide between two shades of gray for the background (this was LITERALLY a gray area: #666666 vs. #999999). Everything else was in place and ONE STUPID COLOR got in the way. A pointless speed bump. In my personal life, I have seemingly replaced *watching a movie* to stream on Netflix with *trying to pick a movie* on Netflix. I pop around "New Releases," "Suggestions for You," every little weird specific subgenre in their thorough suggestion engine like "Italian Vampire Films with Conjoined Twin Protagonists in an Aquatic Setting" . . . Finally, after eighty-two minutes of this, I turn off the TV and go to bed, having watched nothing but previews, descriptions, and 1½ star ratings.

We are so inundated with choices all the time that this abundance of options has actually made our lives MORE stressful. It's easy to fall into a pattern of inaction as we are gripped with the fear of making an inferior choice; pretty soon you run the risk of avoiding decision making altogether because the process is so goddamn stressful. To this day it's difficult for me to play a leisurely game of chess because I can't help but take on the intensity I had when I was a kid. I haven't really tried to rectify this because I don't really care about playing that much anymore. So to Boris Spassky I say, "You are safe for now."

PRACTICE DECISIONS

So how do you get over indecisiveness? Simple. Practice by making insignificant decisions. If I wanted a sandwich, for example, rather then agonizing over whether or not it should be turkey or roast beef, I would just force myself to say "turkey" without thinking about it. Then I would be resolved to be happy with that sandwich. Once I saw that the turkey was a fine choice, it strengthened the emotional muscle that I can make adequate decisions. I realize this sounds ridiculous, but it really helped me a lot. It's rare that you'll have to make that "Lady or the Tiger" door choice. Most decisions we make will result in outcomes that are only infinitesimally different from one another in terms of our enjoyment of them. My dad has the old tough-guy philosophy of "make a decision and don't look back," which can be caramelized with my maternal grandfather Jim Facente's gentle addendum, "Never live with regret."

CHARACTERIZE

 What are some decisions you've been recently struggling with?

 What are the pros and cons of both sides?

YOUR DEFAULT WORD

This might make the more cynical sarcastonauts fire at me with everything they've got. It's a little stunty. I like it, though, because one of the reasons we may not make good (or any) choices on occasion is because we don't have an instantaneous guide to enlighten us in the face of "What should I do now?" One way I've gotten around my indecision is by relying on a default word that I commit to each New Year. This is a word that I want to define me for the year. I do it annually because the Julian calendar is a convenient structure. I decide at the start of the year what I want the theme of that year to be. That way, whenever I get stuck in a situation where I don't know what to do or decide, I think of that word and it almost always makes one option clearer. The word can be a tangible thing like "fitness" or a concept like "superlative." In the case of the former, when trying to figure out if you should have that cupcake for breakfast, your default word might convince you to seek another option. In the case of the latter, if you've worked for eight hours on a project that's due tomorrow and you're ready to give up because "it's good enough," then "superlative" might impel you to put in that little extra bit of work to make it better because your default mental setting is "of the highest quality." Or such a fancy word might make you suddenly don a top hat and perform ribbon gymnastics, but hopefully not. Your word can literally be ANYTHING you want it to be, and you don't have to tell anyone and embarrass yourself, like I just did.

CHARACTERCIZE

 Write down five words that might be constructive default words.

 Pick one that gibes the most with where you want to go and write it under your name on your Character Page.

Remember it in times of struggle.

DECISIONS AND CHOICES ARE NOT TRYING TO MURDER YOU

Your Nerdy brain will naturally want to inspect and assess every option available to you and eventually the crushing weight of this pressure will most likely suffocate you into giving up and proclaiming, "Well, FUUUUUUUCK [insert thing]!" Choices should be a good thing, as I will point out later in the "Confidence Theory" section. Choosing one thing usually doesn't mean killing all of the other options forever. Oftentimes, you can always go back and change your mind if you want. If not, and you realize the decision did not pan out the way you had hoped, you now have a lesson for future decisions. The point is, *own your decisions*. It's not even a mistake: Given all of the information you had, you made the best decision you could. I do this fun bullshitty thing that makes me feel better if I really screwed the donkey in the face with a poor decision. Here's yet another great example! Many of you already know that I'm a huge *Doctor Who* fan. Seriously, I don't fucking shut up about it. In April of 2011, the BBC asked me to moderate a panel with the cast and showrunner Steven Moffat in New York to celebrate the first two episodes of the sixth series of the show. IT. WAS. INCREDIBLE. At the after-party, I found myself in a conversation about British comedy with Mr. Moffat when I realized that I had decided earlier to do a drop-in set at a stand-up show at the UCB. I actually pulled away from a guy whose work I ADORE by saying, "You know what? I gotta run to do a show, but it was really great chatting with you!" In retrospect, this was foolish. Moffat was AWESOME. So many great stories and insights, but that narcissistic comedy gene pulled me away to go hop up on stage for fifteen minutes. Yes! The Monday night UCB show "Whiplash" is trainloads of fun, but I do stand-up ALL THE TIME. How often do I get to chat with one of my genius heroes? I'm not made of synthetic polymers, people! I Nerd out over people as much as the next Poindexter. I kicked myself for DAYS over this until I finally had to construct a bullshit "if-then" situation so my brain would let it go. It went something like this: "Well, IF I had stayed at that event any later, THEN it's possible a meteor may have fallen and killed me on the way home." OF COURSE THAT IS HIGHLY IMPROBABLE. But it's not 100 percent impossible either, and that's how my brain gets tricked. It's a weird, secular outgrowth of my Italian Catholic mother's "everything happens for a reason" thing. (Though don't free will and determinism create a universal paradox? Oh, never mind.) She would always say, "Well, if you had done that other thing, you might have died in a car accident on the way home, so don't feel bad." I added the meteor because large unexplained meteors in urban settings are funny to me for some reason. As ridiculous as it is, it gives my mind just enough of a reason, no matter how stupid, to relinquish its grip on my shame sensors by trumping it with survival instinct. The lower parts of my brain don't have enough logic to know that a space-rock falling out of the sky in New York City at 11:00 p.m. is not very likely. This is because my lower brain is an idiot, but that is its job.

No matter what tricks you use or what decisions you make, go easy on yourself as someone who's on a never-ending quest for improvement. No one sets out to make a bad decision (unless they paid $100 to see Charlie Sheen's *Violent Torpedo of Truth* tour. Right? Who's with me? Remember when that was a timely reference? Aw, man . . . Spring of '11!!! Good times. [chestbump] [woop woop] [crying]).

CHARACTERCIZE

 Write three ridiculous "if-then" scenarios to strengthen decisions you've made.

ENGINEERING LUCK

Luck is an interesting concept. It gets a lot of credit, though some of it is not necessarily deserved. Luck usually gets assigned to other people when it's good, and to ourselves when it's bad. "That jackwad got a promotion??? What a lucky prick!" (Trying to bring "prick" back into style. I mean the word, not the thing.) Or, "I lost my job today. I guess I'm having a run of bad luck." It's rare that people assign the label of "lucky" to themselves, either because they're superstitious when things are going well or they just don't believe they are (no matter how good they have it).

In my experience, there are two kinds of luck: blind luck and circumstantial luck. Blind luck is rare. It is an out-of-the-blue bolt of lightning that has nothing to do with anything other than the alignment of the cosmos in that particular moment (I'm using that astrology metaphor in the figurative sense). Winning the lotto, having a business trip that you didn't want to go on get canceled because of bad weather, answering your front door to find a talking emu who brings you fortune and fame—these are examples of blind luck. Through no action of your own, some really neato thing just happened at you. It's not controllable and you can't force it to happen. Circumstantial luck, however, is far more common and usually mistaken for blind luck mainly because humans by and large are lazy thinkers. Luck in this instance should really be written in quotations, "luck," because it's not an unmotivated happenstance. You have WAY more control over this kind. In fact, YOU MAKE YOUR OWN LUCK. The fortunate or unfortunate occurrences that befall you most of the time are the direct result of attitudes you employ and the choices you make. You set the table every day for what kind of "luck" you will receive most of the time. Architects don't luck into a building. They plan and work every day until it is completed. You are the architect of your life. If your building materials are negativity and inactivity, then you are essentially building a tower made of shit that will come raining down on you in a brown storm of failure. You need strong, quality materials that are well-thought-out and planned. Does this require more work? Yes! Of course! But the rewards are worth it. No architect ever gets all bummed out when he isn't doing any work, like, "Yeah, no buildings just happened today. This SUCKS." They know that it takes consistent effort and focus, not chance.

It's philosophical hypothesis time! Yay! If you're running through a metropolitan area and you get stung by a bee, you might have reasonable grounds to consider this incident "unlucky." You were just at the wrong place at the wrong time and no amount of preparation could have predicted or prevented this from happening. But what if you ran naked through an apiary? If you get stung by a bee or fifty, do you consider yourself unlucky or would you say to yourself, "Yeah, I prolly shoulda seen that comin'." This fictitious stinging was made far more likely by the fact that you actively increased your odds of it happening. I find this to be the way life works: If you're being lazy, eating shitty, putting off work to fuck around online or on your Xbox, you're creating a very nonproductive aura that you may think is invisible but actually floats over your head like a life meter in an RPG. And it's red, which tells everyone that you are "dangerously empty." If this is the case, is it really that surprising that you just got fired? Or that other people are being promoted around you? Or that your significant other took the cat and moved out? I'm certainly not suggesting that everything is your fault, but it's good to adopt the mind-set that crappy things might happen anyway, so why give them any encouragement? When you're making positive, forward-momentum choices in your life, you will be amazed at how "lucky" you get. When you are focused on this idea of good luck, your brain's filtering sensors will not only start to show you "lucky" events, they will also begin to build scenarios that will seem to generate more of the same to justify this focus.

Let's go back to the bee analogy. You're still naked, but change the apiary with bees to an orgy with humans and change the stinging to orgasms. If you're ambling all nude through a sex lounge, you have just crafted a situation where you will probably "get lucky." If you wish to achieve any kind of success in this life, do your best to surround yourself with an orgy of good choices (which you can only do once you accept that having choices is a good thing). This is how you create circumstantial luck.

CHARACTERCIZE

 Write something that happened to you recently.

 Write one way it could be considered bad luck and one way it could be considered good luck, just to demonstrate how perception affects value.

 Write five "lucky" things that have happened to you, then determine if they were blind luck or circumstantial luck.

CONFIDENCE THEORY

Nerds struggle a fair bit with confidence. It's one of the hardest dragons to tame. I've struggled with it my whole life. Why, here's a good Nerdling story for you, dating back many laps around the sun:

When I was in eighth grade, I managed to get a proxy invite

to a party. A kid I knew was going and I think his mom guilted him into taking me. So there we are, at this eighth-grade shindig at some obnoxious kid's house whose parents were out of town (though our parents didn't know that). Of course there was drinking and loud music (I was a stiff kid who enjoyed neither of those things—drinking didn't start until college) and make-out closets and whatnot. We were, to say the least, out of place. We got the weird "Who the F invited you dorks?" looks from people. Remember the scene in *Sixteen Candles* when Anthony Michael Hall and his buddies go to Jake Ryan's party? THAT. Eventually, a spontaneous game of Spin the Bottle breaks out. Up to this point, the pressing of female lips to mine in any romantic capacity was a foreign concept and I was intrigued. Doubly so by the fact that the hottest, most popular girls were in attendance. If a situation could be made of boners, it would be this one. We all formed a giant circle—maybe twenty or twenty-five of us—as the ceremonial bottle dropped in the middle. In a flash of reflected light, it was in motion as it created a tiny glass orb of possibilities. And it landed . . . on Michelle Carter. You know, MICHELLE CARTER. The insanely HOTTEST girl in our class. Only the girl I had lusted over since fifth grade. I wanted her in a bad way, though I wasn't sure *exactly* for what. Had she one day suddenly turned and yelled, "Jam it in!" at me, I'm not convinced I'd have known what to do. (I have a much better grasp on this now, however . . . Sex is that thing where you're naked except for your socks and there's a lot of apologizing, right?) The bottle was spun again. As an altar boy, I prayed to Jesus's father to let the pointy end land on me so I could put my mouth on this girl's face. Clearly, he only half heard me because it did indeed find itself pointing at my shocked and panting face, but Michelle's response was unanticipated. Just as I was in mid-kiss-lip, she pointed at me and shouted, "I'm not kissing HIM," as if the results had included jail time or diarrhea. I was used to public ridicule (once an inventive kid told everyone I fingered his cat. "How long could that follow you through grade school?" you ask. How long could kids follow you around while wiggling their pinkies going, "Here kitty kitty"? Turns out, three years. Kinda funny now that I think about it, though . . .) but this one stung extra hard. Needlesstoblab, it shattered my confidence for quite a while. Like, until college. PLEASE don't say "awwwww" or feel bad. I'm not trying to tell a schmaltzy sob story to elicit sympathy. I'm fine with it. All of that torment made me the person I am, and things are going well these days. I'll cry about it on my bed of cash. At the time, however, any positive emotions I had about myself were cut to ribbons in a tweeny shredder.

Ah, self-confidence. You fickle, fickle slut, you. Sometimes you're there, other times you're with some other jerk, nowhere to be found. The idea of self-confidence is irritating the way it's usually presented, like it's some tangible "thing" you can just throw onto your brain like a jacket. Nerds struggle with this one quite a bit, and all those times when I was younger and felt the pull of social anxiety, it never helped for someone to just say at me, "Have confidence in yourself!" "Is my having confidence in myself helpful toward you fucking off in the foreseeable future?" I would think in my head. What I would *say* was something like, "Oh, yeah! I'm fine! Why, I'm the mutton's buttons!" because I'm not superconfrontational that way.

Lately I've been traveling an ungodly amount, and when I'm unable to affix myself to the Webs, I just drift off into random thought. Sometimes I think about things I have to do, other times I'll relive frustrating situations and get re-pissed about them, and still other times I create fractious, hypothetical situations out of thin air wherein I mentally argue with made-up people in public settings. Recently, however, I somehow fell into a constructive-thought river and started contemplating the concept of confidence. What is it REALLY? How do people get it? Why do some people crumble so easily while others persevere and succeed? Nothing original there, but I had an uncanny feeling that maybe there was more to it than what's on the surface.

Then, while desperately trying to find a cab in another city, it hit me. Confidence in any scenario isn't about trying to convince yourself, "Hey! I'm awesome squared!" *It's about feeling like you have options.* Whenever you have at least one other option in life, you feel relaxed, safe, and cool because if the one thing doesn't work out, you're not going to die. Literally. It's all that limbic system/survival mechanism shit. The brain is more like an avocado than an apple. In other words, layers and layers of higher evolution clamp down onto a still primitive brain stem, and the core of everything we do processes the way a lizard's does.

Using the taxi example, if there were tons of them readily available I would take my time and casually grab whichever one happened to suit me. With only one or even an absence of taxis altogether, I felt desperate and needy. That one damned cab suddenly became *very important* because I believed it to be my only option for moving toward what I wanted. Next comes the what-if game: What if I can't find another one? What if I can't get to where I'm going? The what-if game is largely pointless and stems from panic and irrational fear, i.e., Lizard T. Brainworth. How many what-if worst-case scenarios actually come true? My guess is almost none of them.

"Well, how do I get options if they don't seem apparent?" might be your next question if you bothered to read this far. It's simple: *Strive for excellence in something you love.* When you commit yourself to a higher principle of excellence, there will always be at least one other option for you to fall back on.

Writers, write a thousand more words a day even if you don't feel like it.

Bassoonists, practice an extra hour when your metacarpals are tired.

Roboticists, add a prehensile tail to your robot to make him creepier.

Always try to think BIG PICTURE. How can you contribute more of your talents to the world? Learning, planning, and contribution will fill you with confidence because on a biological level being a contributor lets the world know that you have worthy genes! And when you're learning how to do something you enjoy and ultimately do well, that also becomes mental currency that you can use as armor for a variety of seemingly unrelated situations; and therein lies the cool mind sorcery of it all: The options you create DO NOT have to relate to the situations in which you want to be confident. You don't have to be an ace with the ladies to pick up more ladies—you can excel at something entirely different and still get the action you so richly deserve. The key is for you to feel safe and comfortable.

Options → Safety → Comfort → Confidence

For me, when I have a run of particularly good stand-up shows, I feel like I have that as a cushion no matter how I get rejected anywhere else. The mere option of being able to do comedy fuels my confidence in virtually every other aspect of my life whether it be professional or social. Why is this important? Because the more confidence you are able to cram into your heart, the more you attract good stuff in life. It's kind of a cold economy of nature to reward those who don't seem to need it. I think it stems from the idea that if an organism is strong, it's worthy of passing on its genes. If said organism is desperate and needy, it must be flawed and its spreading must be limited.

So find a thing! Learn it, like it, live it. Give yourself the gift of options. Then bask in the warming cascade of feeling comfortable in your own skin and the good things that await you! Exclamation points!!!!

CHARACTERCIZE

 Write down three things you're good at.

 Think of a situation in which you felt desperate and write down at least two options you might have had. If you can't come up with any, stop feeling bad about it! There was nothing else you could do.

HI, ANXIETY!

Yay! The dark side of being turbo-self-aware and hyperimaginative! Anxiety is your brain turning on you and trying to deconstruct itself. Generalized anxiety is more of a slow burn, where you might feel the dark butt of the universe just sitting on your brain. You might feel hopelessness, dread, or the sense that you might die young. Anxiety is the Great Mimicker and can manifest itself in roughly a hundred different other symptoms, each one designed to trick you into thinking something else is physically wrong with you. It's a bloodthirsty parasite, as the anxiety it seeds creates more anxiety, forming an endless loop of awfulness that sustains and strengthens itself. The physical manifestations of anxiety are truly fascinating. The fact that our brains can manufacture REAL SYMPTOMS that aren't linked to actual maladies is miraculous in its evilness.

A few rad examples are:

Heart palpitations, trouble breathing, dizziness, blurred vision, feeling "foggy" brained, tremors, muscle twitches, electric zaps, confusion, indecision, tightness in the chest, fear of losing your mind, fear of passing out in public, floatiness, nausea, tightness in the head, ear pressure . . .

The list goes on! Hooray! Unfortunately, these symptoms are broad enough that they share common space with the worst

THE WEB: A HYPOCHONDRIAC'S LIFEBLOOD

Please do me a favor. We're friends now, right? OK, good. NEVER go online to self-diagnose. EVER. Don't fucking do it. You might as well just ask Dwayne "The Rock" Johnson to kick you in the solar plexus. Sites like WebMD should just change their name to Enjoy YourCancer.com. There is simply too much symptomatic crossover to make the Internet a place for the untrained Nerd to get accurate information. Even if you're trying to find out why your cheek itches, you'll end up on some kind of British message board with a handful of people talking about how their itchy cheeks led to face cancer. And you'll be convinced you have it. I mean, you ALSO have an itchy cheek. How could it NOT be cancer??? Mainly because you can find out anything about anything on the web, and you stumbled upon the five people in the world who have it. If you think you have a problem, go see a trained physician. You might be a lot of things, but unless you are a trained physician, YOU ARE NOT A TRAINED PHYSICIAN. If your car starts rattling, you don't spend hours in front of your computer reading about how the engine will probably fall out because that happened to one guy once. You get slightly irritated and make an appointment with a mechanic. If you think something is really wrong, go to a doctor. You will see only the worst things online and build a case in your head that you are dying. You're not. You will be OK. You're just too damn creative for your own good!

diseases and disorders you can think of, which is why I IM-PLORE you, as someone who is now committed to mental health, DO NOT SELF-DIAGNOSE ONLINE. [see sidebar immediately!]

Anxiety finds much of its strength in rooting itself in your past or future. "I should have done A." "What if B happens?" A good trick for me was forcing myself to be present. Get out of the nonphysical strata of the other two tenses and live in the present one. Sit wherever you are and notice five things in the room. Study their color, their shape. Do they have a smell? What is it? Experience your surroundings in real time. Do this for fifteen minutes (or longer if you want). This accomplishes two things: (1) It pulls you into the present, and (2) it throws your focus into the external world and out of your internal one.

THE DREADED COOLDOWN

I can tell you from my experience that, as busy as I am, I think I work too much. In trying to accomplish piles of things, try to avoid my mistake. Work is a great anxiety escape for me. It throws my focus onto something else. But guess when I have the most anxiety? During periods when I slow down. Have you ever worked out in the morning (or done something unusually physical), then gone about your day and then only started to notice the muscle twitches when you're lying in bed that night? That's your nervous system finally dealing with the toll you took on it. When you're resting, your body can devote attention to those over-worked areas. I think the same is true with emotional taxation. You never notice how stressed you are while in battle, but then all of the shit you went through has to process sooner or later. I think the best thing to do is not to keep running from it (like I'm so skilled at doing) but rather to let your body deal with it while remembering that it's all just part of the cycle.

The good news for you is that anxiety is not fatal, even though it makes you think it is. It's generated entirely by your mind, either as a reaction to stress or as a distraction. If you're worried about your health—your brain must reason—you can't bloody well worry about the mountain of work piling up on your desk, right??? This anxiety is a created mental state and can thusly be uncreated. Practice mindfulness in the present, slow your breathing, and know that you'll be stronger when it's over (and it will pass). Cry if you need to, scream, punch a pillow—tire yourself out. Just don't let yourself convince you that something is really wrong with you.

Now let's move on to the fast-burn, rocket-boosted form of anxiety that can strike with no warning when you least expect it . . .

PANIC ATTACKS

If you picked up this book I'm going to guess that at one time or another you may have enjoyed the crippling embrace of a panic attack. How could I predict such a thing??? Because people who suffer from panic attacks (I call them "What-the-Shits," as in "What the shit is happening to me right now?!") tend to be smarty-pants creative types, aka Nerdists. I know this because when I initially wrote about this topic on my blog, the response was overwhelming. Most posts will elicit anywhere from seventeen to twenty-five comments from readers. This one had over one hundred. Comment after comment of panic-stricken humans relaying their experiences with a consistent tone of, "Aha! I knew I wasn't crazy!!!"

Folks not blessed with the gift of hyper-self-awareness don't really understand the rush of liquid fear that floods the body. They just think we're being kooky. I have a joke in my act about trying to describe the feeling of a full-blown panic attack: "Imagine being FUCKED in the HEART."

I had my very first panic attack at about age ten. Adorable! After helping to clean out the garage, I had picked up a tray of rat poison with my bare hands and thrown it in the trash. Later that day, after having eaten half a sandwich, I had a shuddering thought explode into the forefront of my brain: *You never washed your hands!* I was convinced that the flush I felt running through my body was in fact poison shutting down all of my vital systems. Fortunately, I'm here to say that it was not poison, or if it was, it was INCREDIBLY slow-acting poison (maybe I should call my doctor).

After that episode I didn't get panic attacks again until college. Unaware of the concept of a panic attack, I was convinced that something was horribly wrong with me and I couldn't leave my apartment for a month. The prospect of having it happen in public kept me under emotional house arrest. It wasn't until a friend of mine pointed out, "Oh yeah, that's a thing. Lots of people have those." The sheer knowledge that I wasn't a freak helped stave off my panic for a while, but every now and again I'd still get the hilariously familiar, "No . . . wait . . . THIS time it's something fatal." I'm here to tell you that not only are panic attacks NOT fatal, but I don't get them anymore. THAT CAN ABSOLUTELY HAPPEN FOR YOU. In this chapter I'd like to share a few tips that I've learned over the years while navigating the anxiety steeplechase.

KEEP YOUR HEART RATE DOWN

This could be the single most important thing to remember. It's easy to believe that panic is purely emotional, but it's not. It's physiological. Emotions may set it off, but once the trigger has been pulled, it's "100 percent pure adrenaline!" as Bodi from *Point Break* would say. (He would also say, "Ayeee am an FBI AyyyGENT!!!" and then we would hold him while rocking and patting him and saying, "Shhhhh . . . *of course you are* . . .") What your body is ACTUALLY plunging into is survival mode, or the classic fight-or-flight response. This explains why you want to punch the air or run yourself into a wall like a *28 Days Later* chimp. This impulse is left over from our forest-dwelling days and is usually reserved for actual life-or-death situations. Think of it as an evolutionary gift that keeps on giving. And giving.

I'm not purporting to have a complete grasp of neuroscience, but if I were to take a guess, I would say that our brain isn't some wonder organ that all of a sudden just appeared from the ether and existed in harmonious wholeness (sorry, Creation Museum). It is the result of millions of years of more and more complex layers lumping over our lizard almonds like a bad spackle job. When you feel that first twinge of panic, your body is asking itself, "Am I in danger?" and for panic sufferers, the answer is usually, "WHY, IN FACT I AM!!!" even though they're not really—the brain is just misfiring, bless it. It means well. It's just trying to protect us REAL HARD. The body then takes us down the adrenaline river ride that we all know and love, shedding our higher brain functions along the way until we end up a heap of panting flesh not knowing which way to run, reduced to lolcat syntax as our means of communication: "Me wan tare skin noff!" It's a survival mechanism with abject terror as a delightful side effect.

Let's examine that first point of entry, "Am I in danger?" Sometimes it might be enough to gently say no, or to at least acknowledge, "OK, I know what this is . . ." But if that don't cut the cerebral mustard try to remind yourself how adrenaline gets through your body: through a fast-pumping heart. That is why it is CRUCIAL to keep your heart rate down. If your heart is slow and normal, you cannot experience a panic attack. It is impossible to exist in both states. Remember, this is a chemical thing. Rather than focusing on how you might really be dying this time, focus on the SCIENCE of what's happening to you. Your instinct may be to fight, but that just makes it worse. Focus on actually making your heart beat SLOWER. Pretend it's a game and first prize is sanity.

AVOID CAFFEINE

As you probably know, panic and caffeine have an electric sexual chemistry: The former comes right after the latter (terrible pun mostly not intended). About eight years ago, my attacks flared up again after having been dormant for some time. "WHY IS THIS HAPPENING AGAIN???!" I pondered over a nice hot cup of coffee one day about five minutes before another one hit. When I went over the timetable of events in my head, there seemed to be a connection. Just for the hell of it, I googled "coffee and panic attacks" and proceeded to enjoy the two million pages that popped up, warning of the atomic dangers of caffeine to the panic stricken. I know, coffee is a bitchin' dominatrix that kicks your ass throughout the day with a twenty-ounce boot, but at what cost? If you can let it go, you should. You will experience almost instant results. Like not thinking you're dying.

BREATHE, MAN, BREATHE!

Just think, if you had a panic attack five hundred years ago, they'd have thought you were possessed by some manner of dark spirit and you would've had the panic burned or bled out of you! Stupid Middle Ages! Today, we know that simple yet proper breathing techniques are helpful with no loss of blood necessary. At the onset of an attack it will feel counterintuitive, but you have to trust that it works. Take slow breaths, in through the nose, out through the mouth, and let the oxygen fill your lungs as you push your tummy out. (Yes, I am a grown man who uses "tummy." I find it more palatable than "food bag" or "shit garage.") This process will help you in two ways: (1) A slowed heart can't pump fear through your body, and (2) the very act of focusing on a measured activity will take your thoughts away from your panic.

Most people breathe very shallowly, up in their chest, and this is very true of panicky types. Especially when you feel your chest tighten. When you take a good, productive breath, your stomach should extend outward because you're getting air all the way into your lungs. When you exhale, your stomach will go back in, pushing the air out. If you can sit quietly for a few minutes while doing this, you will start to feel your chest relax and warm, tingly bits in the pit of your tummy. Imagine those are spreading through your body. You will feel all keen. Remember, you need oxygen to live so get that stuff into you. Take a yoga class . . . learn to meditate . . . buy some New Agey book on breathing . . . play a sitar . . . whatever it takes.

I hope you've gained some insight here and that, if you are a panic sufferer, you know that you have hope, which sometimes by itself is enough to make the panic dragons stop dining on your soul. But keeping that heart rate below NASCAR isn't just for panic attacks anymore! It's also good for quelling anger, hysteria, and just plain old stress (the vanilla of neuroses). Why share my failures and deeply personal experiences with you? Because I want you to feel better. No one should have to live in fear of oneself, ESPECIALLY when the threat isn't real. Don't let your body trick you. Ignore that brain again. It's a process, but you can do it. If you forget any of this stuff in the middle of the night, you can always tear out this page and glue it to your face. Just make sure you don't cover up your air passages. You might have a panic attack.

REEXAMINE YOUR FEARS

Ah, fear. That biological device that's supposed to keep us from running into fire and shark mouths. Unfortunately, it doesn't always do the best job of discriminating between rational and irrational fear. Here are some examples if you're not sure:

Rational: This roller coaster just separated from the track mid-loop. I am now afraid.
Irrational: My foot's asleep. It may be because of a crippling neurological disorder or some type of rare foot cancer.

Rational: I don't think it's safe to eat that bleach.
Irrational: What if I fail at life???

Rational: I fear that if we jump into that lava, our skin will burn off.
Irrational: Everything outside my house might kill me.

Rational fears keep us safe. Irrational fears keep us inert. They usually start with the interrogative what-if and posit the WORST. CASE. SCENARIO. Rest easy because these types of fears almost never come to pass. ("B-b-b-ut you s-s-s-aid ALMOST! That means sometimes . . ." I KNOW! I obviously can't say 100 percent of the time, but just trust that it's a high, high percentage, enough that you should feel OK! [smiley emoticon]) Remember, if you hear hoof clops behind you, it's probably a horse and not a zebra. In other wordsies, it's much less likely that something rare is gunning for you and much more likely that it's something common and harmless. Unless you live on an African savanna, in which case you will probably be assaulted by goddamn zebras. (Zebrae?)

Worry—a gifted therapist once told me—is a misuse of your imagination. It really is the glorious burden of the thinker: We create a problem out of nothing, and then make it as real and horrifying as possible by steering into the worst possible places it can go. The Nerd brain is a fix-it center. It's always analyzing, calibrating, and hypothesizing. Guess what happens when it runs out of things to assess in the external world? IT TURNS INWARD. But think of all of the world-solving answers you could conjure if you turned those outrageous powers onto actual problems! In a pinch, focus on an external problem. If you can't find one, think of something you are thankful for and focus on all ways that it is awesome. If you're not thankful for anything, breathe slowly and focus on nothingness.

Fear! It's learned. It's contagious. It's an asshole! When I was a kid, I wasn't really afraid of much except for Nerd-punching bullies, lightning storms, and the opening title sequence of *Tales from the Darkside*. Then as I got older I began to become afraid of things. It was cumulative. Being afraid of one thing led me to be afraid of similar things. When I was seventeen, I was in an elevator with my mom. The doors took quite a bit longer to open than they should have and I noticed my mom start to tense up. Apparently she had been stuck in an elevator as a young'un and didn't much care for the experience. That tiny moment yanked a cord in my brain that started it like a speedboat: "Yeah . . . what if the doors didn't open?? We'd be . . . TRAPPED!" [cue adrenaline flush and internal scream] Congratulations to me! I was now afraid of elevators. Then I began to think more and more about it—elevators are small spaces . . . being trapped in any small space would be horrifying—voilà! Claustrophobia!!! Since we're on the topic, flying ain't so great either—wheeeeeeeeeeee! The fear had invaded my mind like a termite colony and slowly began to munch away at almost every other part until my emotional foundation was so crippled that, for a period of time in college, I couldn't leave my apartment. It turns out they won't relocate your philosophy lectures to your apartment, DESPITE the very sound argument that representational realism suggests that the concept of "classroom" is defined by the perception of the observer.

As the selection of my irrational fears grew, I realized that they were like a collection of dipping sauces for my brain—all flavor variants of the same basic stuff. One tangy offering that was late to the game was a fear of high floors. If I was able to somehow get past my fear of elevators, the high hotel floor was a neat but separate little fear package waiting for me at the top. My heart would sink into my legs, which would then "gummify," and then the sweating and the hyperventilating would join the party.

Cut to: A few years later when I'd gotten over a lot of my anxiety. I hadn't been high up in a hotel in a while so I had all but forgotten about my fun with acrophobia. Then, I was doing a gig somewhere in the gut of Middle America, which hangs over the Bible Belt of the South while obscuring the penis of

Florida, and was given a room somewhere above the thirtieth floor. When I got into the room and looked out the window, it all came rushing back into my nerve endings. Right on the precipice of panic, I caught myself. I remembered that most of this irrational fear stuff didn't bother me anymore. I fished around in my emotional trunk and confirmed that, no, I didn't seem to have this fear anymore. That was the moment I realized that every once in a while, I needed to reexamine my fears to affirm or deny their presence.

Life is a shortcutting process. In order to take on new tasks and information, it's necessary to create shortcuts for our brain. You ever notice how a lot of elderly folks seem quick to make judgments or stereotype . . . maybe even get a *little* racist as they age? I certainly don't think that's awesome but what could contribute to that is that we have a limited economy of energy. They're shortcutting with stereotypes. Don't we do this with other things in our life (hopefully not the racist part)? Don't we make snap judgments based on little to no information? It seems like too much of an undertaking to put every situation under the microscope and judge it on its individual merits, so we create mental structures in our brain such that whenever we're confronted with similar situations in the future, we can thoughtlessly default to our preestablished idea. I believe fear works similarly, but the fear system takes it one step further because your brain's intention is to try to help save your life by giving you an automatic flight reaction in a crisis situation, or some shit like that. Something happens at some point in our lives and we form a conditioned emotional response. But here's the interesting part: The response will continue to occur EVEN IF THE EMOTIONS THAT DESIGNED IT NO LONGER EXIST. I started to think of it like an abandoned building that still had an active security system—if you trespass on the property, the lights flash and the sirens go off, which would normally scare a person off. BUT, if you just continued to walk calmly into the building anyway, nothing would happen.

As we glide through the Matrix, we change. New experiences spawn new feelings. Sometimes we get over things without even realizing it. The trick is to go back and check every once in a while. Think of it as cleaning house with your negative emotions. It may not always work, but if you could instantly jettison excess fear baggage just by thinking it through, wouldn't it be worth it? SHITYEAHITWOULD.

The next very logical question in your overachieving brain would be: How did I get over most of these fearstuffs? (I say "most" because I still am unwilling to test the boundaries of being buried alive.) It started with a simple decision. I absolutely had to get over them, or I could enjoy a life of self-imposed *Castaway*-ism of loneliness in my dwelling, foraging for crumbs under my stove and carrying on my love/hate relationship with a face-painted volleyball. (Though I would have been smart enough to draw a sex opening on Wilson.) This process was basically two-fold: research and reconditioning. I felt it was important to learn about the concept of fear and the retraining of conditioned responses.

Fortunately, I stumbled across an article in *Psychology Today* that changed my understanding of fear forever. The article stated that when it comes to irrational fear (worst-case scenario stuff) people aren't afraid of things . . . they're afraid of DREAD. We paint ourselves into these nightmare scenarios and allow our brains to run the horror program. "The only thing we have to fear is fear itself" is pretty on the nose. The piece went on to explain that things people really SHOULD be more afraid of, like diet-induced heart attacks, are infinitely more common than plane crashes, but dropping dead doesn't strike the same chord in our brain as a dramatic demise. The message of this article streamlined all of my fears into one manageable mass. I wasn't afraid of a bunch of different crap, I was afraid of ONE THING. Dread. And furthermore, all of that different crap was irrational and unlikely to ever happen. This knowledge alone was instantly comforting. I immediately began working to ebb the dread tide.

BYE, ANXIETY!

Whether it's the fast burn of panic, the slow burn of depression, dread, and overall hopelessness, or some vibrant cocktail of both, it's fixable. I'm not going to sit here and say, "Just think about bunnies!" I would recommend that you get into a therapy program and work with a professional. There is stuff a-brewin' in you and you need to have someone help you pull it out. PLEASE don't worry about your worrying. It is not very likely that "this is just your life" from now on. You just have to seize control and work through it. And you absofuckinglutely can.

CHARACTERCIZE

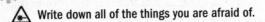

⚠ Write down all of the things you are afraid of.

⚠ See if there's a connection.

⚠ See if you really still feel the fear about each one.

⚠ Write this down and read it when you're in panic mode: "Hey! Wiener! You're just having a panic attack! Count to twenty while breathing slowly! YOU ARE FINE."

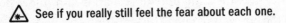

⚠ Then add below it "Baaaaaaaaaaalls!" because that's funny to see written down.

FUN SIDE NOTE!

I am not a professional therapist. I am just a guy who tends to get this delightful brand of brain jolts, so I am merely sharing what I have learned for myself through trial, error, countless hours of therapy, and autodidactic research. Do not *only* listen to what I have said here. There are people out there who have earned the word "doctor" in front of their name. I do not possess this salutation, mainly because I was hosting *Singled Out* instead of getting a PhD. If you need to know the difference between "round and firmy" or "short and squirmy," I am pretty skilled in those matters and would feel much more confident counseling you one-on-one as such. I guess I am also a "doctor" of showing viral videos where people get hit in the nards on *Web Soup*, but that's really only an honorary title at this point.

DOCTOR XAVIERING YOUR MIND

Charles Xavier, founder and leader of the X-Men, has the ability to dig around in people's minds and manipulate them to do his bidding. The concept of mind manipulation has long been a Nerd fave, dating back to teen years when the fantasy of getting to see boobs all the time (which is what a teen mind mutant would naturally use it for) populated many a young fantasy. The truth is, you DO have this ability, *but for your own mind*. I know! I know! It'd be more fun to control other people. However, when you start tricking yourself into becoming the person you want to be, then people might start behaving more favorably toward you, so indirectly it works! And I can promise you you'll get to see your own boobs if you so desire.

There are a million different ways to express hyperbole. Relatedly, there are a million different ways to achieve a goal from a mental standpoint. I think we naturally assume that we have to accomplish the goal for the goal's sake. The truth is, things have no innate value. If you say, "I want a million dollars," it's not the money you want but the feelings it will bring you. Your feelings are rooted in your emotions, and herein lies your ability to play with your motivations. To your brain, wanting a million dollars is meaningless. You have no emotional connection to that.

Consider the following two options:

1. I want a million dollars!
2. I want a million dollars to save an orphanage! (Or replace your nipples with diamonds. Whatever. I'm not judging you.)

In option 2, you've modified your motivation. You're working toward that money for a cause that you care about, not just for the idea of possessing a thing or scratching something off your list. If you care enough about that cause, you'll happily do whatever needs to be done to make it happen.

TWEAK YOUR MOTIVATIONS TO GET BETTER RESULTS

When I was fifteen, I was a part-time caddy at a snooty Caucasian coven known as a "country club." I always hated the job because rich Caucs (I call white people "Caucs") take their golf game VERY seriously, and I always felt tremendous pressure to not upset them by losing their stupid ball because of their stupid slice. Often, I would find excuses not to have to go run around a golf course on weekends like a trained and clothed chimp. I was working for "money," but I only had a vague idea of what to do with it once I got it. That all changed when a guy I sort of knew got a really mega-hot girlfriend. I didn't have a mega-hot anything, so I was intrigued. What was it about this guy?? He wasn't rich (but he wasn't poor either). He wasn't even that pleasant-looking. Rather than credit his personality, I zeroed in on his style: He was a kick-ass skier and had a snazzy pair of Vuarnet sunglasses. It's important to note that I was living in Denver at the time, hence the ski tidbit. My teenage mind reasoned that of the only two things that HAD to make this girl like him, the glasses would be more expedient to acquire than skiing expertise. I became determined to possess a pair.

Sadly, Vuarnet sunglasses were $100, which we considered expensive in those days. Still, I had to make it happen. For six weeks straight, I caddied my ASS off, and happily to boot. Every time I'd get tired or cranky, I'd play through the movie in my head of what would definitely occur once I got those bitchin' eye shields → I'd put them on, walk into the mall, superhot girls would see me walk by, and then sex would start happening on me. (I also may have thrown my thwarting-a-terrorist-attack-with-martial-arts skills into the final edit even though I didn't actually know a martial art.)

That detailed (albeit sadly misguided) cerebral play was the emotional motivation I needed to get through something I hated doing. Not only that, but the snapshot in my mind of that whole scenario took my focus off the dreadfulness of the work and made it FLY by. SIDE NOTE: After a week, I lost the glasses but not my virginity.

STRENGTH AS MOTIVATION

Let's say you don't have a pair of magic sex glasses you want to buy. What if the very reason you did anything at all was because you were committed to the concept of improvement itself? This was one of the things that helped me with my fear of flying. For a while, I was a wreck every time I was on a plane. Deep breaths helped me in the moment, but I was still feeling like I needed to tackle this fear at a deeper level. I wanted to get to a place where the breathercizing (another made-up word) wasn't even necessary to begin with. Something I noticed, however, was that every time I arrived somewhere, I felt a small sense of relief and accomplishment while walking off the plane. I saw this as an opportunity to fuck around with my brain a bit. The direct order "GET OVER FLYING" has zero emotional connection to my brain. The answer it spits back was usually, "No! It sucks. And it's bumpy! I hate it!" Only when I made my goal meaningful did I start to get results. Whenever we'd hit shitty turbulence (which is actually totally safe, BTW), I began to say something along the lines of "Every second you get through this makes you stronger." I was tired of being afraid of everything and decided that I wanted to be a stronger person, and this made my life a septillion times better. This was my emotional connection. It got to the point where I almost kind of wanted the turbulence so my brain could flood itself with reward chemical.

EXPAND YOUR COMFORT ZONES

My flying fear had decided not to confine itself to the aircraft. For many days leading up to a flight I would feel stressed. I couldn't sleep; I just kept feeling the anxiety over and over. If I had written the program in BASIC, it would have looked like this:

```
10 STRESS ABOUT FLYING
20 GOTO 10
30 RUN
```

I decided that my ultimate goal with flying was the experience of carefree travel. I wouldn't feel the crescendo of pants shitting leading up to and including (not literally, of course) the flight itself. Instead, I would be comfortable, and almost a little— GASP—*excited* to fly. Rather than being subservient to my brain, I took little bits of control at a time. If I started the freak-out seven days before traveling normally, I would instead devote the seventh day to relaxing, breathing slowly, imagining myself comfortably flying. Then I'd allow myself the old pattern starting on the sixth day. Taking little bits of control in this manner was not only easier than just getting over flying all at once, but it started to lay an emotional foundation of strength with the new pattern I was trying to establish. No, this is not a quick fix. No, it's not revolutionary. But it worked. Today I'm relaxed to the point that I get sleepy the second I step onto a plane.

Expanding your comfort zones doesn't have to just mean facing fear. Your career should be one big comfort-zone-expanding sphere. Actually, your LIFE should be one big comfort-zone-expanding sphere, if you want it to be interesting and fulfilling. Tiny example here → I am a terrible guitar player. I can play some chords, but I'm not great. Earlier in the year I decided I wanted to do a song for a show at the San Francisco Sketchfest (sfsketchfest.com) = BEST comedy festival in the United States. The problem is, playing in front of people is entirely different from playing in your home. It's a whole separate learning curve. At first I shot down the idea in my head. "I could NEVER do that! I'll suck!" But as soon as I said that, I got all up in my own business and said, "All right, Assy, now you HAVE to do it." So I started doing the bit at small shows around L.A. And guess what? I sucked! But also guess what? IT WAS GREAT. Liberating. I was terrified to do it and I did it anyway. It was awful, but it was by no means a failure. The worst thing that happened was that I messed up a couple of times, and it turns out that's not so bad. And when I saw that I could get through it, I felt energized by the experience. I got better, more comfortable, until SF Sketchfest finally arrived, and I played that goddamn song in front of four hundred people. Body armor. It's hard to be down on yourself when you spit in anxiety's douchey face.

CHARACTERCIZE

 What are some things you're afraid of doing?

 How could you expand your comfort zones?

GETTING UNCOMFORTABLE: YOUR PERSONAL R&D

You are basically an intricate company, so let's say if you devote 90 percent of your energy to maintaining current projects, seeking out new business, and marketing your product, the remaining 10 percent should go to research and development. This will keep you relevant and ensure your steady evolution as an entity. Things are either growing or they're dying. Be a grower. [snicker] To grow, *you must stretch your boundaries.* Boundary stretching will always feel slightly uncomfortable. Slightly uncomfortable is GOOD. Seek out the unfamiliar and the uncomfortable. I don't mean to seek out misery. It's more akin to that feeling in the pit of your stomach when you went to your first school dance or the first time you picked up a game you'd never played before. You will feel clumsy, confused, and lost. If you stick with it, however, you'll quickly recognize the patterns and the details that ultimately lead to your conquering it. Think about it: If you're a gamer, you don't just play the same game all the time forever. You play, you master, and you seek out new titles to repeat the pattern. (Obviously networked gaming and MMOs offer constant change and challenge, so don't throw *Halo* or *WoW* at me to try to discount this idea.)

Uncomfortable = New Experience = Growth

Of course this is scary! Of course it's risky! But the payoff is worth the risk. No one ever became great seeking only comfort (except for the guy who invented the Snuggie—honestly, wrapping up in one of those is like being in a three-way with two angels). You will fall. You will get up. Then you will fall less. Then you will feel your universe widen and you will be a better human. If you know that you're committed to growth, then falling on your face isn't so bad. You can leap up like a mad professor and say, "Aha! I knew it! There was too much drag on that design! Back to the lab for readjustments!" Then you can build a lab and grow out your hair in a wiry fashion to complete the whole Mad Professor aesthetic. I began to more fully embrace the trying of new skills when I asked myself, "Would I rather protect my ego or do stuff in life?"

CHARACTERIZE

 Write down five new things you could try.

 Build a mannequin replica of yourself so you can chestbump it.

EXERCISE YOUR EMOTIONAL MUSCLES

The habits you form and the grooves you settle into are not at all unlike the muscles in your body. The more you make the same choices in one direction, the stronger the emotional connections to those things become, and subsequently the weaker the opposite directions become. It's like building up XP in your Character Tome. For instance, let's say you're afraid of flying. Every time you consciously make the decision not to fly because you're nervous about it, you rack up another few points' worth of fear. As the months bleed into years and you have an exorbitantly high number of these points, the more you have strengthened this association and the idea of even looking at a plane could make you instantly shit your pants. I knew a girl who had developed such an insurmountable fear of snakes that you had to refer to them as "S's" in conversation because she couldn't stand to even hear the word. This is the result of a lifelong fear workout.

FORTUNATELY, you can change your deepest beliefs about something by exercising your emotional muscles a little bit at a time. If you're in terror mode even thinking about flying, close your eyes and get a still image in your head about what freaks you out. It might be horrible, but just freeze it there. Now, with the picture clearly in your mind, imagine a Photoshop-like interface overlaying it. How would you want to change the image? Make it smaller? Erase out the flames? Fill the plane with cats? Make your changes and then do a mental "Save As . . ." Flying. Or S's. Or French clowns. Or whatever paints your nightmares.

For me, manipulating the image in this way gave me a weird sense of control over the situation. Granted, emotional responses are pretty dang fast, so it probably won't change in that moment, but if you keep going back to it little bits at a time and playing with it, your feelings will start to shift. Don't feel like you've gone back to square one if you have another freak-out after doing this for a while . . . It's all part of the "forming new associations" process, and this would be where you reexamine your fears from the previous section to make sure you still have the data in your brain to support the level of fear that you're manifesting. You probably won't, and you'll be back to where you left off in no time.

CHARACTERIZE

 Write down something you're afraid of.

 Write something good or beneficial about that thing.

 To go one step further, draw your worst-case scenario.

 Now change the drawing to give it pleasant imagery.

LOOK FOR GOOD NEWS

Do you have that one poisonous friend who seems to THRIVE on delivering bad news? Just like the very first Debbie Downer sketch on *SNL* (ONLY the first one—you can delete the subsequent ones from your mental file tree). People LOVE giving bad news. They love it. This is because negative information GREATLY empowers the giver and makes them feel important. Why? Because we listen. It affects us. Also it's rude to respond to someone who's just told you about something terrible in the following manner:

A Veterinarian: Your cat, Mr. Boots, has feline AIDS.

You: . . . Aaaaaaaaaaaand?

This is what the news media has become. Something that tells us daily that our cat has AIDS. Or that murders are up. Or that a common household item could possibly kill you. Bad news always gets more weight. We pay more attention to it because it feels more real for some reason. So then what starts to happen? We expect more bad news. When we do that we start to see more bad news. Once we get used to seeing more bad news we begin to actively seek it out. Sunshine is boring to us. You know how younger girls tend to screw the grease-enhanced jerkwads who blow them off rather than the nice guys who show up on time with flowers and mix tapes? We are exactly like those young girls but with news instead of jerkwads: The more awful it is, the more we want to get it inside us. And when we build our worldview around the idea that we live in this fucked-up vortex of despair, it weighs on us even when we don't realize it. The response to my recent panic attack post was overwhelming. As I sifted through the comments and emails I received, I felt like I noticed a recurring theme of "I don't know why but I've been getting more panic attacks lately." Naturally, I have an unsolicited theory: I think the present mondo-Apocalypto POV in our country is largely to blame, and it's fired into our faces EVERY DAMN DAY by the tragedy whores of the news media.

WE GET IT. THERE'S AN ECONOMIC CRISIS. WE'RE IN A DEPRESSION. They even went as far as to inform us, "Hey, remember 2007? We didn't know it then, but that was a depression, too!" just to make sure that any recent memories were also charred in the magma of despondency. WAR, DEATH, NATURAL DISASTERS: the manna of the media. You think all of that blackness running in the background of our emotional desktop isn't going to have a profound effect on our mental state? OF COURSE IT IS. Yes, it's important to be informed about the world, but it's ALSO important to keep in mind that it's not all horrifying. NEVER forget that news shows and newspapers are run by companies that survive on ad sales driven by ratings, and the best way to achieve that is to keep you crapping in your Dockers so you'll tune in. (That part's actually OK. You should've gotten rid of the Dockers in '99.)

It is therefore entirely your responsibility to make yourself feel better. No one's going to do it for you. That sucks but sometimes you gotta work for things worth having. That is why it is imperative that you do the following: LOOK FOR GOOD NEWS. I know it's campy and hokey, but I believe it to be vital to your emotional survival. You don't have to go on some kind of doe-eyed Pollyanna bender; just start out by taking five minutes a day to find something about the world to feel good and/or hopeful about. I googled "happy" and found HappyNews.com, a site devoted solely to positive news stories (but if you Google "good news" you may accidentally enroll in Bible college). As I tooled around the site, I swear to you I felt better inside—and I'm normally one of those cynical comedian types.

Read good news. Hug a flower. Look at a puppy. Doesn't matter. Just create a space in your soul for hope. Remember earlier? *The reality you experience is almost wholly shaped by your perception of it.* YOU HAVE THE POWER TO CHOOSE WHAT YOU NOTICE. You know how you have that one friend who only dates douche bags? How could she not see what a piece of shit that guy is??? She's choosing to notice different things. I don't recommend doing this with a douche bag, but you should certainly do it with life. I'm not saying you have to believe that everything is awesome all of the time, but at least start to open the drapes in your brain and let some light in. Once you do you'll get addicted to it and you'll start to see the good in things (a good skill to have). That isn't New Agey crap, that's brain science, people! If I said to you, "Hey! Wingtips!" you would start to notice wingtip shoes everywhere and wonder if they were always there or if they coincidentally just started popping up. (I would then ask you why you lived in a 1930s gangster movie where wingtips are so plentiful.)

I'd go even further to assert that if the media started reporting that the economy was turning around, people would start to unconsciously make it happen. Tensions would relax and consumer confidence would begin to increase because they would start to look for reasons to do so. I'm not advocating living in denial, but I am saying that there must be SOME good stuff happening. Why can't we throw some focus on that? It would CERTAINLY help put us back on the right path. Things being as they are, however, that may not happen anytime soon, so the onus is on you.

If you try this with some consistency, I guarantee it will ultimately affect you in ways you cannot imagine. It'll be like pulling back the curtains and letting in some warmth to the dark recesses of your soul. But be patient! You will not change overnight! A jetliner can't just flip a bitch—it has to turn into an arc and slowly make its way around to go the other direction. The same is true for your perception. Shape your reality. Don't be a pawn for the darkness. Find the good news and what motivates you and inspires you.

Always remember that you are not a helpless victim of your emotions. Long ago you may have given up control of your brain and set it on autopilot either because you didn't know you had another option or because it just felt like too much work. And it is work! But for me, this work was well worth it for the prospect of not waking up sad every day.

CHARACTERCIZE

⚠ Write down five outlets that can be your go-to places for good news every day.

BREAD CRUMB YOUR LIFE WITH MUSIC

Every year on my birthday I start a new playlist titled after my current age so I can keep track of my favorite songs of the year as a sort of musical diary because I am a teenage girl. Making a greatest event list each year is also useful (more about that later), but sometimes looking at words isn't necessarily enough to transport yourself back to key life moments. In my estimation, mp3 players are the closest things to time machines we have. A good song woven into the fabric of space-time is a bread crumb that maps the trail of your life. If there's something that you listened to every day five years ago, and it happened to punctuate a particularly good time in your life where you felt great and made what you considered to be excellent choices, listening to it again will access the emotional files from your mind's root directory and pull that mind-set into the forefront of your brain. Here's one of mine:

1 "Yankee Bayonet" ....The Decemberists
2 "Young Bride" ....Midlake
3 "Mike Mills" ....Air
4 "As We Go Along" ....The Monkees
5 "Don't Hesitate" ....The Procession
6 "678" ....King Creosote
7 "Look Up" ....Zero 7

8	"Phantom Limb"	The Shins
9	"Street Spirit" (Radiohead cover)	The Darkness
10	"The Age of Elegance" (The *Prisoner* theme)	Ron Grainer
11	"Last Love Song for Now"	Okkervil River
12	"California"	Rogue Wave
13	"Up on Crutches"	The Sea and Cake
14	"Bodysnatchers"	Radiohead
15	"The Sulphur Man"	Doves
16	"Backyards"	Broken Social Scene
17	"Spare-Ohs"	Andrew Bird
18	"The Bones of You"	Elbow

For instance, track number 3, "Mike Mills," accompanied me through Europe one year. I have very strong associations with it being on a train from Venice to Switzerland, one of the most breathtaking experiences of my life. Now, I don't want you to think that I think you're an idiot. OF COURSE you know how music works. YES, you already know it brings up old feelings. My point is that by structuring it in your life as a musical diary or log, you can control your feelings and change them on a dime if you need to. Oftentimes, people don't think to do this and only get affected if a song comes up on shuffle. If you want the super-Nerdy analogy, imagine that each song is a Horcrux, which contains a tiny piece of your soul that you can scatter and map out in the world. And you don't even have to perform *Avada Kedavra* to do it! (Hey, where's everyone going??? [dejectedly stuffs wand back into robe sleeve])

ADDICTION-ARY

This chapter may not be for everyone. If you don't feel the nagging tag of addiction, telling you to partake of substances that you know in your higher brain are bad for you, then skip this part! I don't believe that everyone who drinks is an alcoholic. There is nothing inherently wrong with alcohol. If you can do it responsibly, drinking is like pouring smiles on your brain! Also I realize that addiction can cover a wide variety of flavors encompassing food, drugs, the Internet, drama—whatever. Almost anything is obsessable. For these purposes, though, all I can do here is talk about some of the stuff I went through, and you can agree or tear these pages out and wipe your butt lips with them.

I will say, however, that it's my guess that a lot of Nerds suffer from addiction. We are a group that obsesses over things, dives into things to the level of *Abyss* depth, and has a very active internal monologue. These are some delightful ingredients—mixed with a bit of genetic predisposition—for overdoing things that make us feel good in the moment. For me, it was all about drinking. I was never really able to smoke the weed or do hard drugs. The few times I did the former, I had panic attacks because I thought that my heart would stop beating if I didn't concentrate on it (this is a strong deterrent). The latter I avoided altogether, my thinking being something along the lines of, "If I can't handle pot, a drug that is supposed to mellow you out, then something like cocaine would probably make me feel like my internal organs would want to exit my body all at once via my skin." The fear of leaping into traffic during a narcotic-induced freak-out was enough to keep me away. Beer, it turned out, made me feel like I was in control, which was a big thing to me. Many Nerds led tumultuous young lives. Besides being a bit smarter than their counterparts, many Nerds are socially ostracized. I believe that because the Nerd is not being sated in the external social world, he or she is forced to turn inward. I don't think this is necessarily a bad thing, in that it paves the way for self-awareness and introspection. You know how some of the popular kids in school seemed to lack substance? This is because they were not in a social stratum that forced them to search themselves to find any. Many of their grade-school successes were predicated on the fact that they were accidentally attractive or rich or outgoing. Jocks live in an external world. They don't plot. They don't plan. They just act. Many of these types grow up with an unearned arrogance that will either further their aggressive-bastard quest into adulthood, or destroy them when their external qualities begin to fade and their lack of depth renders them emotionally unarmed, and without the necessary tools to cope with life.

Nerds, on the other hand, are HYPER-self-aware, as I have previously stated—sometimes to the point of being unhealthy. For me, drinking beer was a way to silence this awareness, or at least take it down a few notches. For others it could be pot, eating, drama (yes, some folks are hopelessly addicted to creating drama), whatever. I think it all comes from the same place. We have difficulty controlling our brains and we get into a pattern of gaining control artificially. Ultimately for me, I think a lot of it had to do with control. Nerds LOVE control. They crave it. Eating a shitload is a form of control over your body. Video games are chance to control a universe. Never striving for better in life is a way to control your outcomes: If you don't try, you can't be rejected. Whenever I could fire a regular stream of beer into my gaping maw, I knew exactly how I would feel, and that was usually pretty good—in the short term. Short-term-benefit actions are fine sometimes, but certainly not ALL the time. Today's spontaneous feel-goods could be tomorrow's failures if you let them dominate your life.

Addiction is a tough one. It tricks you. If I were to try to explain it to someone (people who don't have the gene can't fathom it), I would say that it's like having thousands of hungry baby birds in your soul, chirping and begging to be fed on a molecular level. It's hard to deny them and they can be very persuasive. If a dog begs and begs and begs at your table, sooner or later you might just give him a bit of steak to shut him up. It's less painful in the moment than exerting all of the energy to retrain him, but that's what you need to do—retrain your soul. To do this, you need a plan and you need support. Personally, AA never resonated with me. I'm not proud or ashamed about that. It just was what it was. For a while, I thought I was REALLY broken until another comic friend of mine said, "Yeah, I didn't really like it either. I just kind of did my own thing." Then a light went on and I felt OK. Now, many people from the Program will balk at this. I have a friend who occasionally will ask me, "You still not going to meetings?" to which I always say, "Naw, they're not my cup o' tea," to which he'll reply something along the lines of, "OK, Champ, good luck with that." Well, I've been sober for eight years so my "luck" is holding pretty well. As alcoholics, we tend to be self-centered, so it's difficult to imagine that something that worked for us might not work for another human.

BTW, I'm not bashing AA in the least. For some folks, it's a lifesaver. They need that specific structure and that system. I only mention all of this because if you happen to be someone who didn't click with it, I just want you to know that you're not a loon or alone (that's some snazzy wordplay there!). Having said all of that, I cannot express to you enough the importance of SOME kind of help. I had a therapist that I was crazy about, so that worked for me. An experienced friend can also be helpful. Or the AA route. Also, I haven't used it, but I recently discovered a social network for those in recovery at IntheRooms.com that looked promising. They allow you to connect with similar folks at varying stages of recovery to give you support at any level of privacy you prefer. However you go about it, know that you just need some kind of wise, guiding force. You see, the substance isn't the problem. Substances are things and, by Nature, innately neutral. They are an expression of an underlying emotional or chemical issue. Your job in recovery is to try to dig that up and somehow sign an armistice treaty with it. I've seen so many people who quit doing whatever it is that they do, and think that's going to solve their problem. Quitting only provides the clarity to discover *and then* start solving the problem. These can be troubling waters to navigate because several years of artificial coping may have stunted your emotional growth. I became INCREDIBLY emotional in the beginning because it had been so long since I had to just use my own brain to deal with things. It's like that scene in *The Matrix* when Neo first gets rescued and he's on the operating table looking like a pincushion, and he says to Morpheus, "Why do my eyes hurt?" "Because you've never used them."

START WITH VANITY

Vanity should never in and of itself be a goal, but we all have it so we might as well use it. A lot of people ask me how I was able to quit drinking on October 8, 2003. (They don't cite the date. I added that for dramatic effect.) The truth of the matter is, it started as vanity. I wasn't working. I was fat and doughy. My skin was bad. I looked like death puked on a turd. The year prior to that (I believe), I was watching *The Daily Show*—as I was wont to do—and my old TV mate Jenny McCarthy was a guest. Near the end of the interview, Jon Stewart goes, "Oh, by the way, Chris Hardwick works here now." "Really? Cool!" Jenny responded. Stewart quickly shot back with, "Yeah. He gets our coffee." [big audience laugh] Fu. Cking. BALLS. I had just gotten called out on one of my favorite shows for being a loser. And the worst part was, *he was right*. The rush of embarrassment and self-awareness forced me out of my body for a minute, giving me a CRYSTAL CLEAR view of my surroundings: I was holding a beer, which was about to join its several empty compatriots on the table in front of me. There was a pizza box. I was in my underwear. With no shirt (it was on the floor nearby). The only thing that could have made it sadder was if the cops from *Cops* kicked down my door for some reason and pinned me to the ground while upbeat reggae music played. I would be surprised if Jon Stewart had any recollection of his off-handed flèche, but I owe him a debt of gratitude because it was the first time I actually said to myself, "Uh . . . this may not be the best way to be living, young man . . ." I had hopes! Dreams! Desires! And they were CERTAINLY not fail-y crapsack desires. I knew there were two pathways I was staring at: One choice allowed me to continue drinking every day and eating pizza every night until 4:00 a.m., but I would probably turn into a blob who never worked again and became that sad story of the guy who used to be on TV before he got all boozy and gross (which was already happening). The OTHER choice held a lot of mystery, but it was an intriguing mystery that at the very least could give me a fighting chance.

The first thing I noticed about sobriety? I lost about twenty pounds within a couple of months. I started getting compliments. This was HIGHLY motivating. Years later, and through much therapy, I would come to discover all of the REALLY bad things alcoholism caused, like anxiety, paranoia, and perpetual emotional infancy. But it all started with vanity. If you're having trouble getting over something, try motivating yourself through this method. Find a reason to change that calls your vanity or ego into the mix. If you're a thinker, you're most likely a bit selfish and I don't mean that in a negative way—but if you're always in your own head about stuff, you can't deny that you're focusing on yourself a lot, and how the world sees you. It can be hard to connect to the "you should get over it just because" line of reasoning, or even a "do it for the kids" mentality. We are self-centered creatures and by nature will usually put our own happiness/ avoidance of pain first. Use it to your advantage. Altruism is challenging. Selfishness is innate.

The same lost souls who ask me how I quit also inquire as to how I was able to make it stick. It's a daily choice I make, I suppose. Not in the sense that I think about it every day—I really don't. But on some level, a choice is made to not pour many beers into my bloodstream. The first prong of this choice is in the acknowledgement to myself that I can't drink responsibly. In 2003, the last year of my Olympic-grade booze consumption plan, I decided that I would try to "cut back" (mainly at the behest of others). This lasted a day. Then I moved on to, "I'm going to stop for thirty days just to prove that I don't have a problem!" It is my belief that if this oft-uttered sentence leaves your mouth, you have a problem. The reason is, people who don't have the drinking gene don't think about drinking in quantifiable terms. Even if you DO quit for thirty days (which I had failed to do at the time), you're still thinking about it the whole time and how much you're going to "fuck shit up" on Day 31. It's not in the activity of sucking down the booze that alcoholism lies, it's in the mental fixation on it, usually as a means to a numb end. You see, fair and curious reader, I can't say what it's like for drugs, but with alcohol I always managed to find a way to weave it into every activity. I drank socially, I drank when I was depressed, I drank when I was happy. For me it was a way to never feel anything too much; this, I discovered, was the result of a much larger avoidance on my part of ANY responsibility, whether in the external world (I had ruined my credit from being a lazy bill payer) or the internal world, where I just didn't want to have to deal with emotions of any kind. I remember exactly what that felt like, and I absolutely don't want to be in that space ever again—that is the second prong. I never miss drinking, but while on vacation in Italy a few years ago, the thought of having a beer in the first-person-shooter-like streets of Venice just sounded nice. Then I walked myself through the result of such an action: I'd probably have a drink or two and guess what? I'd be fine. No dark genie would shoot out of my nose and eyes and take me on an immediate bender. In fact, I might not drink again for a week. Then I'd be somewhere else and think, "You know? I was fine before. I'm sure it's fine now," and do it again. And then again, and then again, and then again. My guess is that it would probably only take three months to get back into peak condition as a full-time beer-thelete. Because I'm able to walk myself through this process and know unquestionably how it would turn out, I choose not to do it. I'm able to not drink because, oddly, I respect the strength of my addiction. If you'd like to see a visual representation of how the unleashing would play out, watch John Carpenter's *The Thing*.

The other thing I pass on to sober n00bs is the importance of good friends. How can you tell the difference? A bad friend is one that says, "Aw man (or lady or lady-man)! You don't have a problem! Just come out with us!" With these assholes, you need to hold up your crucifix and garlic and back away slowly into the daylight. The good news is, once you quit drinking you probably won't hang out with these douche chimps anyway, because your relationship was based on "going out." A GOOD friend will say something along the lines of, "Whatever you need, I'll help you." The day I got off the sauce (October 8, 2003, in case you forgot or stopped caring), my bestest fwend in the whole world, Mike Phirman, said, "Hey! I'll not drink too if that helps!" My mom cried when I told her that. Had I the capacity for basic human emotions at the time, I might have as well. He never put an expiration date on the offer. He could just not do it. I couldn't fathom how that was even possible, but those lucky dorks without the alcohol gene can just take it or leave it. It is also worth noting that Mike is a friend who should be bronzed. Maybe not literally, as from his point of view this might not be viewed as a reward, but I know that part of my success in sobriety was because of a guy like Phirman, and if you're looking to make strides in your sobriety, you NEED friends who are not connected to you through tributaries of booze. But stay away from Phirman. He's MY friend. Get your own fucking Phirman. Also you should buy his solo comedy album at MikePhirman.com because it is awesome and you deserve at least SOME Phirman in your life.

CHARACTERCIZE

⚠ What do you think you might be addicted to?

⚠ How much of your life revolves around your finding ways to in-corporate this into your life?

⚠ Write down the things you do to engage in this behavior.

⚠ Some key points if you think you have an addiction:

⚠ Decide that you want to deal with it—it will never stick until you do.

⚠ Get counseling.

⚠ Use vanity for good.

⚠ Avoid the substance of choice or any social situation that would take you into your old patterns.

⚠ Respect your demon.

⚠ Make good (new if necessary) friendships.

⚠ Make the daily choice for a better life.

⚠ Find a Phirman.

⚠ Send me $100,000.

⚠ Ignore that last point.

SUCSTRESS

You know what sucks? When things don't go your way. You know what else sucks? When they actually do. It's a weird thing, but getting what you want can actually be stressful. I call it "sucstress." If you put yourself out into the world in a creative way, you're going to face a lot of rejection. It's just the nature of the beast. And what you do with that rejection matters. Use it to inspire not to enfeeble (thanks to Merriam-Webster.com for the antonym assist). What can happen, though, is that you can get used to rejection, so much so that it feels alien when something goes right. And if a BUNCH of things go right, you might have a freak-out. It's so bizarre that in a time of great success—that thing we convinced ourselves would make EVERYTHING better—we can experience *more* stress than we do in rejection.

Things You Might Say during a Sucstress Freak-Out:
1. "OMG. Something terrible HAS to happen now! I'll just brace for the other shoe to drop." (See Irish Catholic joke from Chapter 3.)

2. "Is this really OK? I mean *really* OK? No. People weren't meant to get what they want!"
3. "Well, it's only a matter of time before I fuck THIS opportunity in the face."
4. "I finally got what I wanted!!! But . . . what if something takes it away?? What if I get maimed in a terrible accident??? NOOOOOOOOOO!!!!!"

Things You Can Say to Your Brain in Response:
1. "The Universe doesn't work that way. To the Universe, positive and negative values only matter when referring to particle charge, not human events."
2. "Yes. It's foolish to think we exist here to toil in misery."
3. "That will only be true if you decide to believe that, but it doesn't have to be."
4. "The right thing to do is to enjoy the fruits of your labor. Sweat-fruits, I call them, for no reason I can recall. Honor your work as if it were a person you respected."

You might engage in any of the former thoughts for any or all of the following reasons:

1. You don't think you deserve nice things.
2. You're addicted to despair.
3. You're Catholic.

A horrible thing to do to yourself is to wake up in the middle of the night and imagine all of the horrible things that can take away the good things you have. It plays out in Oscar-worthy, cinematic fashion in your head. For me, it was (and sometimes still is) a movie where I get terminal cancer. Right at the moment where my life is where I want it to be. "WHAT A SHAME," everyone says. I see myself, curled up and sobbing in a hospital bed—it's all over. All that's left is the dying and the greasy feeling of unfairness. The dark parts of my brain direct the action independently of my Will . . . They loop in my mind and swirl like a turbulent weather pattern, increasing in vividness and detail with each new screening, upshifting my heart like a Formula 1 car until I am in full-blown panic mode. Have you ever felt that? I hope you haven't. But I'll bet you have.

So what can you do? I've found the best way for me to pull out of this aggressive nosedive of awfulness is to not fight to shut the images off, but rather to take control of the direction. Steer the images into something impossible, ridiculous even. The more stupid the better. What I do is (and I'm slightly embarrassed to admit this) to "arborize" myself. I made up that word because I don't know what else to call it. I go back to the horrible scene in the hospital bed, and I imagine my feet sprouting roots, my hands growing into tree limbs, my body spurting out leaves . . . It's admittedly weird. Kind of makes me sound like a psychopath to see it in print, but the effect is golden. I've taken a scenario that my brain thinks will happen and shifted it into the realm of the impossible. My brain instantly drops the emotional connection it had because it can't reason such happenings.

If you do it, get as creative as possible. Turn it into a fun thing. Honestly, the weirdest shit you can conjure: break-dancing meerkats, clouds raining penises, people shitting out rainbows— whatever. Just make it weird.

CHARACTERCIZE

 Come up with a ridiculous scenario to play during sucstress freak-outs.

THE COMFORT OF REJECTION

Having been socially ostracized since early childhood, most Nerds are very comfortable with rejection. Not that we love it or anything, it's just that it's familiar. *Not* getting rejected is unfamiliar, and we fear the unknown. It's a dumb survival thing. Your short-term-planning lizard almonds will ALWAYS SEEK OUT COMFORT. They want to please you in every moment. However, you are not a chimp. You have the ability to override your brain and plan for long-term happiness even if that means discomfort in the present. Here's how it might go down:

1. Things are going better than they ever have.
2. You wake up one morning strangely depressed.
3. The rest of the day you don't feel right in your skin.
4. Dread and doom set in.
5. You begin subconsciously dismantling your success while sprinting to get back to your previous comfortable state.

In this moment, take a deep breath and let yourself understand that you are just experiencing growing pains. It's SUPPOSED to happen. It will pass if you let it, and you will soon feel "normal" in your better environment. Again, please don't think that I mean "money" when I talk about "better environment." That should translate to "an improved position from your current one." This can be a good relationship (for once), a better job title, a more advanced group of work peers, even the freedom of retirement. "Better" often feels "new" and new situations are like jeans: They can sometimes take a little bit of time before they start to fit right. If ever there was a situation to pursue the uncomfortable, this is it. In this case, being ACCEPTED for your talents is uncomfortable but definitely worth overcoming. I had to realize that believing that I would only know and deserve rejection was a thing I made up in my head. Fuck off, brain! Maybe not surprisingly, things started to go better more consistently once I did.

CHARACTERCIZE

 Write down five positive things your newfound success will bring you, and let yourself FEEL them.

 When you do begin to achieve success, who do you want to be? The act of succeeding itself will not make you happy forever. Don't think it's going to suddenly make everything rosy. It is a good thing but it's not a magic spackle for your problems. You come out of success with the same emotional baggage you had going into it. If you're unhappy in life, work on that separately.

THE POWER-TRIPPING NERD

Beware! Because Nerds tend to experience rejection from a young age, they tend to skew a little on the crazy side when they finally achieve success and power. Go easy on the little-brains.

You don't need to destroy them like rodents in a crush video. Be thankful and gratified enough by your success. If you treat people like shit, they will revel in your demise if you ever happen to slip up, and getting back up to Castle Awesomegaard can be a bit more challenging the second time if you've burned all the bridges leading to it.

We (myself included) seem to live in a constant state of "If I just had X, things would be RAD." We tend to live in a constant pursuit of happiness, as defined by exterior goods or circumstances. I think pursuing happiness is the wrong approach. That idea puts it into the future, and therefore in the wrong tense. You just need to BE happy—in the present—with who you are and what you have. I realize it's not as easy as flicking a switch on and off, but my point is that having a bunch more stuff isn't going to fix you. You have to do that through reflection, assessment, and appreciation. Steal moments of happiness if you have to, and then collect them until they are the dominant images in your psyche. If your computer blue-screens, you can't dump a pile of money and tits on the casing and expect that's going to get it working again. You need to go inside, figure out what's wrong, and repair it. (It's probably the logic board.)

THE THIRD REACTION

Some Nerds are timid when it comes to anger and confrontation. Others have itchy rage triggers because they have spent their lives fighting upstream socially and therefore have some control issues. I am one of those people. I don't get pissed at important things, mind you. Just things like computers, traffic, and telephone customer support menus. Occasionally I'll get snippy with another human when they probably don't deserve it. Nerds know they're smarty-pantses—in fact, it's part of how they define themselves, so sometimes we come from a place of "everyone is stupid but me." This is shitty and wrong. It also leads to spontaneous emotional reactions to situations rather than calm, well-thought-out ones. Here's a little trick to keep you from going from zero to yelly in 5.4 seconds: *Whatever your first reaction is, make it your third.* Look, if someone's giving you the guff, you shouldn't be afraid to stand up for yourself and tell them what's what, but oftentimes this isn't necessary right away. In Stephen R. Covey's *7 Habits of Highly Effective People*—a title that is so sterile I'm sure it was thought of in another language initially, then translated to English—one habit is "seek first to understand." This is GOOD. Real power is controlling your emotions, not letting them launch whenever you get an urge. Your knee-jerk reaction is usually more about you than the situation at hand. Before leveling someone with your loudness and clever barbs, try to understand the issue FIRST and discuss what options might help you fix it. If that gets you nowhere, regroup and seek a levelheaded resolution a second time. If you're STILL getting an unfair roadblock, then you can shoot your anger load all over everything as your THIRD REACTION (but not in a physical way, of course). If you can do this, you will cut down your outbursts by about 90 percent and in that gain real understanding and solutions rather than ignorance and enemies.

The Nerd mind is a powerful and complex machine. The fact that you have a lot of internal struggles is actually a gift because it means that you have more going on inside than most. You're extra-special, and sometimes that's hard. It's the burden of being the smartman that you are. The good news for you is that BECAUSE you're a smartman, you can—and oftentimes will have to—outsmart your brain. It might seem like a hassle, but Uncle Ben Parker was right on when he blabbed about great power & great responsibility. Enjoy the fact that you have both!

Congratulations for getting through the first section! Give yourself a whopping 50 XP in your Character Tome!

PART TWO
BODY

YOU START NOW

THE NERD PHYSIQUE

"Emptier than a hotel gym at Comic-Con" was a comparison I made about the Kardashians once. That's a twofer, one of those analogies that's mean to every referent it contains. Truthfully, I don't know the Kardashians. They might be nice. They're just an easy target and I was being a dicknose. Nerds and comic cons, however, I AM intimately familiar with, and many of them are not in awesome physical condition. I know! I get it! I was always picked last, too. And begrudgingly at that. In fact, when I was in eighth grade, they made me take gym with the fifth and sixth graders. (Awwwwwwwww.) It's no wonder with this kind of youth-based failure that I would have had negative associations with fitness later in life.

The Nerd body isn't necessarily one physical type. It can be large, small, fat, or freakishly skinny. The constant is that, by and large, Nerds do not feel comfortable or coordinated in their own skin (except the fingers, where the game controlling lives! UP-UP-DOWN-DOWN-LEFT-RIGHT-LEFT-RIGHT-B-A). *How could I make a blanket statement like this?* Am I just an arrogant D-pad? Possibly. But I've also lived with Nerds my whole life. I attend cons every year. I see different regional Nerd packs regularly, and I know this: Body language doesn't lie. Nerds slouch, they won't look you in the eye, they stare at the floor mostly, and they seem to be on a mission to wrap their entire bodies around the center of their chest. I think there are two forces at play here that contribute to this slouchtopia: (1) Humans who aren't comfortable carry themselves in a very closed-off, protected manner that pulls their shoulders forward and their heads down, and (2) years and years of sitting at computers or in front of video games have created the standard binary slouch. In other words, any device that has a binary-based system will almost always make you hunch over to interface with it. When most of your time is spent slouching, your body just assumes that position no matter what you're doing.

In pursuing fitness, you're pursuing knowledge of your body machine, comfort in your skin, and a natural confidence in your interaction with the world that will pull your shoulders back and allow you to expose your chest, a PRIME symbol of "shit's cool." I'm not telling you to become a 'roided-up monster, but I believe that everyone deserves a little "shit's cool" in their life.

WHY???

"What is this jock bullshit? Fitness? Body? Why are you rolling this wheelbarrow full of feces at me? Am I supposed to buy into this, you asshat? And when did I become so aggressively inquisitive??" I THOUGHT ALL OF THESE THINGS, TOO. For years, physical fitness equaled "dudes." Dudes lived for sports. Dudes pushed people around. Dudes chestbumped during cheerleader threesomes. Dudes were barely literate and could not see the inherent value in a Labor Day *Twilight Zone* marathon. Here is a not atypical exchange:

> **Me:** . . . So when Burgess Meredith emerges from the bank vault to a post-apocalyptic world and shatters his glasses, he is unable to consume the books that were his only passion, therefore imprisoning him in irony . . .
>
> **Dude:** I see. [punching starts]

Naturally it was my instinct to reject all of their habits and behaviors. I had become proud of being out of shape. "Yeah! It's a choice I'm makin'!" I'd say, as the dough piled on around me like an inner tube that was being custom fitted for me. "I don't NEED their shitty ways. I gots beer and late-night cheeseburgers." I can't tell you how many times in my twenties I would order a pizza after coming home from bars, eat half of it, pass out, and then adopt the rest for my breakfast the next "morning" (at 2:00 p.m.).

Say, that's all well and good for your twenties because your body is much more Wolverine-like up to that point. Guess what happens in your thirties? Your mutant X-Men gene shuts off and your body starts expressing the horrible things you're doing to it. I'm all for everyone being happy with who they are and stuff, but that comfort level diminishes exponentially as you age into worse and worse shape. I once heard comedienne/actress/loud-talking gadabout Mo'Nique (I still don't understand the apostrophe's role in making that name function) say something along the lines of, "All those skinny bitches can go to hell. I'm fat and proud. I'm comfortable with who I am!" I agree! You should like yourself for yourself. If you're overweight and you're happy, then that is what's most important. "There's nothing more attractive," my brilliant writer pal Brad Meltzer once said, "than someone who's comfortable in their own skin." But if you are seriously over-weight, just make sure you really understand the health risks as you age. Let's check in again when you're fifty, sixty years old (if you're lucky and don't drop dead of heart failure first) and your mobility is greatly decreased because of poor circulation, ankle strain, or—gods forbid—a diabetic leg amputation. How com-fortable might that be? You shouldn't have to be model-skinny. In fact, models are fucking freaks—anomalies, really—that shouldn't define the image ideal. You should, however, be healthy and trim enough that you can enjoy the flexibility to make it to the bathroom by yourself with both of your natural feet when you're older.

Also I take umbrage with the concept of "being content with oneself." It's bullshit. You should be HAPPY with yourself. Contentment is a sedentary state. Taking care of your body is the best way to express that, not filling your mitts with a wad of cupcakes and saying, "This is who I aaaaaam!" while spitting out crumbs and jimmies. It's not who you am. You am a good person who deserves to feel good in the long term. Taking care of your-self will accomplish this. And you don't really even have to do this all of the time! You can do it some of the time and still come out ahead! You don't have to eat like a triathlete unless you want to completely transform yourself. You can make slight improve-ments and reap benefits.

When I started exercising in my early thirties, it was really an investment in my future. I didn't want to hit fifty-five and go, "Gah! I'm a twisty, weak, hardened wreck! Better start this ex-ercise process!" I believe it's never too late to start, but it's a shit-load harder to try to throw the ship into reverse in your senior years. I had this weird goal that I wanted to hit fifty feeling good and looking younger than my quinquagenarian counterparts. You know those old people who look like someone mashed up a bendy Gumby figurine and just left it? Most of this is nothing more than lack of even light, consistent motility. When you see that, do you ever have the somewhat dark thought, "Shit . . . if I end up like that, please take a bat to my head, Universe." I have spoken to elderly folks, and more than one has expressed regret at not taking better care of their teeth and their body. The beauty is you don't have to ever worry about the bat option if you just do a little prep work now, while you still can.

When I was eighteen, I was in a really bad car accident in which a transverse process of my fifth lumbar vertebra was cracked. If you know the spine, you know that's a deep injury. Because I never did any physical therapy to strengthen the sur-rounding musculature, I had excruciating back problems for fifteen years. Like, the kind where sometimes you can't walk without leaning on a cane while expelling the most colorful string of swears in your vocabulary. (I became very creative. Who knew the C-word had so many applications??) I reasoned that this may not go away on its own, as age tends to slowly prey on our weaknesses until it stands triumphantly over our petrified bodies. I wanted this not to happen, or at least, I wanted to know that I did everything I could to prevent it. This was another rea-son I started taking my physical health seriously.

My final reason for hopping on the exercise train: I was a card-carrying member of the "I'm a Lifelong Pussy" club. I hated confrontation (as most Nerds do) and had this aura about me in which I carried myself like I was about to get beaten up in any given minute. Nerds of my generation were flinchers. If someone jumped at them even slightly, a spazzy flinch would be the result. I was over it.

I am here to tell you that it was one of the five best decisions

I have ever made. Not only am I healthier and younger-looking than I was in my twenties, but my back problem is pretty much gone. I say "pretty much" because when I don't stretch or exercise for a couple of weeks, it gets tight. "Does this mean I have to do this exercise shit forever??" Number one, don't think of it that way. "Forever" anything is just too overwhelming for the human mind. Number two, yes. Yes, you should if you want to feel good, which is way worth it in my book, which is this one incidentally. Additionally there are things you learn about yourself when you exercise your body regularly that are applicable in other areas of your life—things like pushing limits, setting goals, being committed to something. These may look like dumb words and the concepts are difficult to understand on a visceral level if you haven't done it, but I promise that if you take your physical being seriously you will have aha lightbulb moments regularly.

Over the years I had joined gyms, let the membership lapse. Rejoined them. Joined different ones. Had trainers. Bought fitness books. Used them to even out table legs. Given up. Then, in 2005 I met the right guy. He was a "dude," but a good dude. He changed everything for me. His name was Tom (and still is, not surprisingly). My girlfriend at the time had been going to Tom since the previous year and loved him. She met Tom through our mutual friend Gabe who also was a client. Gabe and Tom met in perhaps the best way possible: WHILE PERFORMING LIVE *STAR TREK* EPISODES. Gabe played Spock, while Tom tackled the academic brogue that was Scotty. This was actually the thing that piqued my interest to meet him—a classic Nerd connection.

Many times my gf had come home extolling his virtues: "Tom is the BEST. It was so amazing today." They HAD to be porking, right? "Amazing" is an orgasmy word. SURELY she couldn't be talking about working out, which as we all know is a painful, awful process that only psychotic people endure. Well, not being the jealous type but still intrigued by their connection, I came up to meet Tom one day while dropping her off. Tom's a handsome man. A few years older than me, good posture, square jawline. To look at him, you'd never assume that deep inside beats the heart of a guy who wants to be a Nerd. (Tom has a deal with one of his many tech-head clients wherein they trade training sessions for Photoshop lessons.) "Hey! Janet said you might be in the market for a trainer," he said in a boyish, enthusiastic manner (but NEVER forced or annoying), which I would come to realize was his charming default setting.

I was sort of in the market for a trainer. I had always been a scrawny kid. I was four-foot-nine my freshman year of high school, at which time I began to grow until I hit five-ten by senior year. Still, I was about 125 pounds, so no one was ever in any danger of being harmed by me in any physical way. In my twenties, the drinking and late-night pizza consumption had chubbed me up to about 170. When I disembarked from my booze-cruise lifestyle, I had lost roughly thirty-five pounds within a few months, but I was not in good shape. I was just skinny, but in the way that I looked weak and slightly ill. More than one of my comic friends posed a variation of the question "How's that [insert terminal illness here] coming?" (It's not offensive if you understand inter-comedian humor.) It was time for a change. I've always been jazzed by the idea of reinvention (though usually not by the word "jazzed" itself)—the idea that we are not petrified chunks of matter but rather balls of moist clay that can be remolded many times throughout our lives. I wanted to not be a weak wiener anymore. I also was on the other side of thirty and realized that most dudes in their thirties UTTERLY let shit go. It's usually where the unraveling starts, and the last bit of physical activity they engage in is the act of throwing in the towel. I felt a weird competitiveness with ALL DUDES MY AGE. I had this idea that I wanted to live the rest of my life as someone who you couldn't really tell how old they were. I reasoned that a fitness regime might help this.

"What type of training have you had in the past?" Tom asked. Naturally, I tried to make it sound more intensive than it actually was because I'm a guy and we are adept at posturing. "Yeah, I've been doing a bunch of boxing training." This was PARTIALLY true. The "a bunch" part was questionable. I had gone to a place in Hollywood in an old mini-mall called Wild Card Boxing Club. It was divey, pretty much an enclosed prison yard. The fascinating thing about it, though, was that it was THE REAL DEAL. The gym's owner, Freddie Roach, is a world-class trainer who has worked with the absolute biggest names in boxing, many of whom pop in from time to time. Wild Card is a place where a prep school kid like me would slightly fear for his life, but if you're serious about the sport, it's a good way to go. I enjoyed the few times I went, but was too intimidated by the skill level of the other combatants to muster up the gumption to keep going.

"Great!" Tom said. "I've been a kickboxer and martial arts guy for twenty years! If I train you, it'll give me a chance to dust off the ol' mitts!" "Well, I dunno . . . I'm kind of busy these days . . ." (I wasn't.) "Look . . . I like you. You seem like a good dude and I think the world of Janet. Just gimme a chance. I'll even train you the first time for free. I am confident that I could change your life." It didn't sound sales-pitchy. There was kindness in his voice and sincerity in his eyes. "Oh, OK. I'll give it a shot." Six years later we're still training together.

Tom trains out of his modest loft dwelling that I would later dub "Apartment Dojo." His workouts are a mashup of boxing, weights, cardio, and stretching. No two workouts are ever the same. This was very helpful in keeping the sessions interesting. His philosophy revolves around always keeping it fresh, and pushing your brain into new territories so you never get too complacent. It's stimulating both physically and mentally. Also our sessions have become therapy sessions. If I'm having a crap day, I'll tell him when I arrive. At the end of the workout, when I'm stretching and completely spent, Tom will wryly ask, "So were you able to think about your day?" The answer is no. A good workout is the most constructive distraction from the rest of your life. This is part of the package deal that comes with Tom's main goal for each workout he's constructed for you, which I will blab about in the next chapter.

THE GETTING-OFF-
YOUR-BUTT PART

It is time. Your butt has been magnetized to the opposite polarity of your metaphorical couch for far too long. The planning, the putting off, the waiting for some "day" or "thing" to happen to get you started is now. If you think about it, you'll talk yourself out of it. You have to act in defiance of your brain, which you learned to do in the last section. You also might find yourself in the "I don't know how or where to start" bin, which is a sentiment that is truly the thief of so many good things that never got a chance to happen. Should you join a gym? Should you get a trainer? How do you even find one those people? Should you train in a Siberian barn during a *Survivor* music montage like in *Rocky IV*? Let's have the first of many chats with Trainer Tom!!

A Q&A WITH TRAINER TOM FOR YOU, THE INQUISITIVE READER

At the writing of this book, books are not sentient beings that will field your specific questions. I'm sure you have many, and since these papery jerks are too fucking stupid to answer you, I will step in. "How do I find a good trainer??" Were you wondering that? If so, I rule. If not, I drool. Nonetheless, you should want to know that before you put your physical well-being and money into some stranger's callused paws.

Below is a Q&A with Trainer Tom to help you vet potential trainers.

ME: How does one find the best trainer?

TOM: "What's the best kind of martial art?" or "What's the best karate school?" in the past. I have always answered with the same metaphor: If you were going to send your child to school, you would go and meet the teachers, sit in on a class, and get the vibe of it. Same answer for seeking out any school, trade, and even a trainer. I've always said, "There are good plumbers and bad ones. Keep looking till you find one you like!"

ME: So my trainer needs to be a licensed plumber? Tom, I'm confused.

TOM: First and foremost, anyone can kick your ass, beat you up, or work you till you're sick. That has never been a goal of mine when training anyone—EVER! Nor is it at all impressive. To me it shows a lack of what a trainer really, truly needs: a complete understanding, empathy, highly developed communication skills, and the ability to relate to anyone's circumstance and train them as individuals with individual needs, rather than "This is how I do it and this is how my clients will do it." It should not be about the trainer. It should be about you.

ME: Tom, you have provided me with the clarity I was so desperately seeking. What else should I look for once I've found a cat I click with?

TOM: They should be certified. It does not mean they need a large number of acronyms behind their name. But at least it will show that they didn't just decide yesterday to try and be a personal trainer.

ME: WHAT IS THAT OVER THERE???

TOM: Where? (Tom turns. I snatch some of the roasted almonds he has with him.) I don't see anything.

ME: Oh. Nothing. Must have been a ghost panther or something.

TOM: O . . . K . . .

ME: How much of my hard-earned or inherited money will I spend on a fucking trainer?

TOM: Call a few gyms near you and find what the going rate is for a trainer. Just because a trainer charges a lot doesn't mean they are good, and vice versa! Also if you find a great trainer and can't afford him, well, it won't matter then either. Find what you can do, manage, and afford.

ME: Some people tend to get nervous at the mention of personal trainers. Why do you think this is?

TOM: Many people who have not worked out before are the most vulnerable to or fearful of a personal trainer. My first session with every client, no matter if I know them or not, I always say the same thing, "On a scale of 1 to 10, this workout will be a 4. While I get to know you, I will also be getting to know your body. Anyone can kick your ass. Tomorrow I want you to feel like you worked out, but be able to say that that wasn't so bad, I'd do that again! To me being user-friendly is the only way to get people started. Once they begin to become familiar with me, working out, the steps they must take, the sacrifices they must make, and the rewards that will follow, they are normally hooked and truly understand that they are the true sole recipient of all their effort.

ME: Will books ever be sentient?

TOM: Not in our lifetimes.

continued

ME: What's your favorite monotreme?

TOM: The echidna.

ME: If Commander Riker beams down to a Class M planet, which crew members does he need to take from the NCC-1701?

TOM: That's a trick question. The *Enterprise* from *Next Generation* was the NCC-1701-D.

ME: Well played, you clever bastard.

TOM: That wasn't a question.

ME: [falls out window]

If you're serious about getting into shape, a trainer is someone you should STRONGLY consider having in your life. It's not only about having a professional who can guide you, but also about the concept of being accountable to someone. If you're spending money and someone else's time, you are more likely to follow through than if you only had to answer to yourself about scooting your nuts to the gym. And "But I'm broke!" may be valid, but REALLY think about it . . . How much money do you spend going out to bars a couple of nights a week? It's probably about fifty or sixty bucks. That's what I was able to swing (actually more) when I was professing my brokehood to my fellow college goers. You will almost always find little bits of money for things you really care about. Now it is time for *you* to be the thing you care about! (OPRAH MOMENT ALERT: Audience "awww-wwwws" and music swells as we throw to a douche commercial.)

START SMALL-INCREMENTAL CHANGE

The biggest problem with sweeping change is that it's sweeping change. Change is work, and massive change is sometimes just too daunting and runs the risk of putting us in "I would not like to start that shit right now" mode. Here's a suggestion: INCREMENTAL CHANGE. Just alter one habit or behavior SLIGHTLY and see what happens.

Six years ago, when I started working with Trainer Tom, I was convinced that it probably wouldn't last. I had been to trainers before who were "all in to win" guys. They told me up front that I had to train at least three or four days a week or I shouldn't even bother. Well, those guys can suck it a lot. Tom was smart about it. He knew what would happen if I just tried exercising one day a week: I'd start to feel a little better, so I'd gradually want to do it more. One day a week pretty quickly turned into two days a week, which then became three after six or eight months. Once here, it occurred to me that if I ate a bit better, the workouts would be more effective. The addiction to feeling good I had craved for so many years through artificial means was now aimed at accomplishing the same thing through healthy, natural ones. Then I actually began to seek out my own fitness OUTSIDE of Apartment Dojo, and now I can't imagine going more than a few days without some kind of physical activity.

If you know you should eat better, try doing it just one day a week. The other six days you can dump sugar into your mouth until your blood caramelizes. This is more of a manageable chunk, and doesn't rip you away from your other habits too abruptly. (Obviously, if you feel you have a serious chemical addiction, seek PROFESSIONAL counseling and not just the advice of the *Web Soup* guy.) We love to talk about the butterfly effect in terms of time-travel movies: "If you change even the SMALLEST of things in a system, its long-term effects can be dramatic." Why can't the same be true for lifestyle changes? Don't you think you would be better off even if you only lived well one day a week for the rest of your life? Chances are, it won't only be that one day. You'll feel better, get stronger, and seek out more of the same. Before you know it, you'll have eased yourself into a far superior habit string. The best analogy I can think of is bank interest. It only seems like a few percent here or there, but over the long term it's the compounded interest that any obnoxiously wealthy person would happily tell you was one of the contributing factors to their wealth.

Start with incremental change. You'll get used to it. The key to *Homo sapiens*'s survival all these thousands of years is our ability to adapt. Just as you got into a groove of treating your body like shit, so will you acquire the desire to hug it.

FEAR OF "GETTING TOO HUGE"

When I first started working with Trainer Tom, one of the things I said was, "You know, I've thought about working out in the past, but I just didn't want to get too huge." Tom chuckled. He knew this was a common excuse for people who simply didn't feel like working out. Here are some analogies to that statement:

> "I was worried if I got my driver's license I'd start winning all the NASCAR races."
> "I was worried if I got a job at Safeway I'd end up owning all the Safeways."
> "I was worried if I started putting ice in my drinks I'd deplete the world of its entire ice supply."

The people who are "too huge" have to work out as a full-time job, eat INSANE amounts of protein (like twenty chicken tits a day), and/or take supplements of varying types. I work out two or three days a week and I am by no means huge. I'm just fit, and that's good enough.

Honestly, you don't even have to exercise that much to completely change your life! Do it once a week, maybe twice. And you don't have to crush yourself each time. If you're starting from nothing, a half hour on the treadmill a couple of times a week is a wonderful place to start. It's the consistency that matters. If you do it regularly, you'll be amazed at how quickly you feel better, AND to your surprise, you will start to crave more physical activity as you move forward.

If you're not gung ho to completely alter every aspect of your life at once, a philosophy of incremental change is a good way to go. Massive change all at once has a higher failure rate. Do you play guitar? If not, go out and learn guitar for this next analogy. I'll wait. [pause here]

Hey! How was learning guitar? Are you rad now? GREAT! Actually, what I'm about to say has very little to do with the actual playing of the guitar, so I may have led you astray by telling you to put your life on hold to be awesome at it. It's about sudden change. When you restring a guitar, it falls out of tune very quickly. The strings are tight and need to loosen up over time into their new positions. A little twist here, a little tweak there done consistently, and you'll stay in tune longer. Know that the more you try to change at once, the more challenging it will be and the quicker you might fail. It's OK. You wouldn't put new strings on a guitar, tune it once, and then yell, "Well, fuck THIS noise!" when it's out of tune ten minutes later. You know that you are committed to breaking it in and keeping it in tune. We are all like guitars. (Especially because the lengths of our necks and sizes of our holes vary. #HEYoooooooooo #HashtaggingOutsideOfTwitter)

ALWAYS LEAVE FEELING BETTER

"PUSSY! Here's a tampon to soak up some a those tears!"
"But my back kind of hurts."
"No pain, no gain! PUSH through it!"

Cut to six-week injury.

How many times has this kind of trainer prevented someone from EVER wanting to work out again as long as they live? Trainer Tom always stresses SAFETY in his workouts. He stresses proper form and control to avoid injury.

Trainer Tom also taught me the value of goal specificity. Yes, yes, we all want throbbing guns and rock-hard abs if every issue of *Men's Health Magazine* is to be believed. A shredded eight-pack is a difficult goal to achieve, and equally difficult to maintain. It's not impossible, but if you're committed to a life of decent fitness, your long-term sights should instead be set on having a high quality of life. The first thing Tom said to me when we started working out together was this: "No matter what, I always want you to leave feeling better than when you arrived." What? No 'roid-induced aggression? No screaming? No nitro-powered cock punching??? "Nope. I'm going to teach you how to hug your body." Good! I think it's tired of being dietarily and sexually abused by me. I am willing to stop ONE of those things.

And this simple philosophy, "Always leave feeling better," is a slight twist on traditional exercise regimens that has helped me go from a ropey guy with no flexibility and a bad back to a guy who's in pretty dang good shape with no back problems. When your specific pursuit is feeling better, you usually FEEL BETTER. This is addictive. I began to seek out other ways to feel better: regular massages, yoga, eating better, stretching. The results are similar to having a hard-core man-goal. The exercise does get me into better shape, I just don't get hurt in the process. When working out, it's good to test your limits. Remember, the things you learn in your workout space you will take with you into the world. Sometimes this means going past where you thought you could go. This does NOT mean pushing through body pain. Your body has a very loud voice when injury is afoot. LISTEN to it and don't try to be a brainless Hulk. The Hulk, at his core, is really just a personified erection. Regardless, he has an infinitely dense molecular structure thanks to an accidental overdose of gamma radiation. You are a breakable person.

When I walk into Apartment Dojo, the first question I get from Trainer Tom is "One to ten. How do you feel?" Based on my honest assessment, we work out accordingly. Some days that means high-intensity moving and weights, other days I feel like punching so we break out the gloves and pads. (Yes! I kind of know how to box now. Notice that is distinctly different from knowing how to FIGHT. If I'm in a bar and someone shoves me and then holds up two pads, I could hit them. All day long. If they start swinging at me, however, there would be a lot of crying and fear-pee.) Some days, if I've been traveling a lot and my body is tight, we just stretch. And I leave feeling better than when I arrived.

BTW, I *cannot* emphasize to you ENOUGH the benefits of stretching. Honestly, if you do nothing else in your life, regularly getting blood to your extremities and loosening your musculoskeletal system by even fifteen minutes of stretching in the morning and at night will do you wonders in this life. It not only improves flexibility, which will help prevent injury, but it also gets blood to your muscles. You know how you do that beargrowly "yeeeeARRRRRRRRRRRG" stretch when you first wake up? That's your body instinctively forcing blood to your extremities. Oh sure, an elderly existence of being gnarled up and hardened by years of atrophy and stiffening SOUNDS like a rad plan, but I'm sure it is not. Here are some examples below, provided by Simon the Workout Bear:

Important Stretch Points!
- Do it slowly.
- Don't rock your body to stretch more.
- Be gentle.
- If it hurts, stop; don't try to stretch through pain.

More stretches can be found at NerdistWay.com/Stretches.

". . . AND NOW A WARNING??!!"

I love the Zemeckis film *Death Becomes Her*. The second after Meryl Streep downs the eternal youth potion, Isabella Rossellini says, "And now, a warning . . ." Streep flawlessly shoots back, " . . . and NOW a warning??!" It's funnier to watch than to read, I know. Still, I feel compelled (mostly by our litigious American society) to disclaim the following section a lot. In mere minutes, you will be carried through the shiny showroom of physical fitness. The workouts and eating tips are *suggestions*. They should get you moving in the right direction. Obviously, everyone's biochemical makeup varies, and I cannot stress enough to you how important it is to work with a trained professional one-on-one who can tailor a program to your specific needs.

The stuff here should get you started, or at least thinking about it. People hurt themselves in gyms because they don't know or understand the mechanics of their bodies and pull or wrench too hard in the wrong direction without realizing it. Don't be the injured sobbing person at the gym. It's what the jocks expect of the Nerds. Please do all of the fitness/diet stuff AT YOUR OWN RISK. You'll notice that there are three workout sections, because my lifestyle is such that I need workouts that are suitable for (1) going to a gym, (2) working out at home, and (3) working out on the road (usually in hotels). The next sections were written based on a combination of my own workouts and a rigorous interview session with Tom in which I denied him both food and water and ensured the safe return of his Chihuahua, Mija, if he cooperated and offered you, the Nerd reader, the highest-quality fitness information.

Enjoy! (Safely.)

WORKOUTS

If I have time to do nothing else, I'll stretch for ten minutes. If I have slightly more time, I'll do cardio. Even twenty minutes is better than no minutes. For me, twenty minutes of cardio at a light run with varying inclines every five minutes is a great way to maintain a decent level of fitness. If you want to start somewhere, this is a good place. Your heart lives to pump blood through your body, so doing that faster than resting state a couple of times a week will start to condition it to handle more stress. If, in addition to the cardio, you can fit in a workout once a week that targets the muscles, that's even better. However, it's often less easy to figure out a workout than to step outside or onto a treadmill for a power walk.

AEROBIC VS. ANAEROBIC EXERCISE

The science-y, college boy, gonna-get-whupped-in-a-redneck-bar answer is that aerobic exercises are fueled by oxygen and anaerobic exercises are fueled by a source other than oxygen, namely glycogen, which is basically unused glucose stored in your muscles and liver after breaking down from carbohydrates. No-carb diets are dangerous if you're trying to build muscle, because carbs provide the fuel to do it. Distinguishing the two types!

Aerobic
- "Heart-pumping" exercises
- Running, jumping, spinning, swimming, Riverdancing
- Longer intensity

Anaerobic
- "Muscle-building" exercises
- Weight-lifting, machines that cause resistance
- Short bursts of intensity

A good, well-balanced exercise regime utilizes both. If you lift weights one or two days a week, consider doing an aerobic exercise one or two of the other days for maximum efficacy. NOTE: You don't want to lift the same muscle groups too much in a week. Muscles need adequate recovery time to strengthen. Breaking up your workouts in this manner will help ensure that you do this! *A good rule of thumb is to wait forty-eight hours for a muscle group to fully recover.*

TO QUOTE LAWRENCE THE CABLE GENTLEMAN: "GET HER DONE"

To give you one less excuse, the following are three workouts Trainer Tom (or Tom Weights, as I sometimes call him) has come up with for you. They are good, generic places to get you in the fitness door if you've been outside pressing your face up against the glass for a while. Since aerobic exercises are slightly more intuitive, Tom's starter program is going to be in the ANAEROBIC (remember thirty-five seconds ago?) category. My workouts with him are usually thirty minutes straight, during which I am constantly alternating the muscle groups being worked. If I need to catch my breath, I'll grab a sip of water or do some microstretching in between moves, but generally I go from one exercise to the next right away. Tom also changes the order every time. In all these years I can honestly say I've never had exactly the same workout twice. This shocks your muscles and keeps you from getting too comfortable or complacent. It also keeps you from getting bored.

It is also worth noting that these exercises can be used by both men AND women and possibly some third, as-yet-to-be-discovered sex. The reps, or repetitions, can be the same for everyone. The variable will be the weight you use. And your potential for asexual reproduction.

WEIGHTS AND MEASURES

It's a generally accepted rule that if you want to tone your muscles (pronounced "mus-kulls," à la Popeye), you'll want to use lower weights but higher reps, and if you're looking to pack on meat, heavier weights but lower reps. Don't worry about meat-packing right off the bat. The truth is, you have a huge potential for growth anyway if you're a beginner because you've never really used those areas before. The following is a good, basic starting table:

Muscle Area	Male	Female
Arms/Shoulders	5–8 pounds	3–5 pounds
Chest/Back	10–15 pounds	5–8 pounds

This, however, is just a guideline. Your individual choices should be based on your comfort level and ability to do each motion comfortably and correctly. Tom emphasizes this and has therefore NEVER had a client injure himself or herself in twenty-five years.

You will see rep suggestions listed below each excercise. Don't kill yourself to meet them and don't cheat with poor form to eke out those last few. It's OK to go to failure. "Failure" here means "until you can't do any more reps with good form," or more specifically "muscle fatigue." "Failure equals success in workouts," Tom always says. In other words, it's not the number that counts. If all you can do is five reps, then your muscles are being worked to their limit. If that is painful for ANY reason, next time try a lighter weight.

LINE → SPEED → BEAUTY

Tom ALWAYS advises going slower and lighter in the beginning. When I first put on gloves and started flailing my arms in a boxing-like attempt, he told me, "Line. Speed. Beauty." In other words, get the basic form down slowly FIRST so you can see how it feels. *Then* you can jerk off your ego by showing how fast you can do it. THEN you can worry about making it look perfect and seamless. This applies to lifting weights, or any exercise for that matter. Go slowly and constantly check in with your body to make sure nothing hurts. ALWAYS focus on good technique first. Even if you can only afford a trainer one time a month to keep you on track with your technique, it's worth it.

NONLABOR CONTRACTIONS

When lifting a weight, it's all about those contractions, or the squeezing of a muscle at the peak of the move. So let's say you start with five-pound dumbbells. If you can do fifteen to twenty reps of that, huzzah! Stay slow, keep practicing your form, and keep your body still. If you're curling, for example, you don't want to be shifting your body around to help you complete the move. The movements should be localized to your target area. This will prevent owies. You would curl the weight up and give the biceps a little extra squeeze before lowering it. Nothing violent or aggressive. You're not trying to attack yourself or freak out other people at the gym.

If you can easily do twenty to thirty reps with the five-pound weights, congratulations! Now start the process over with eight-pound weights. These may sound light, but if you're doing a high number of reps with proper form, you will be AMAZED by how heavy eight pounds feels. As such, the highest weight Trainer Tom has on his weight shelf is twenty-five pounds, and I have never felt like I needed any more than that.

POSTURE

This will be tricky for Nerds. We have notoriously bad posture. When lifting weights, it's a good rule of thumb to remember, **"Sluts Ferociously Bite Big Sausages, Then Lick Balls"** (or SFBBSTLB).

S: SHOULDERS back.
F: FEET shoulder-width apart.
B: BEND a little at the knees to take the strain off your back.

B & S: Keep your BACK STRAIGHT (i.e., don't hunch; keep your spine in a line).

T: TIGHTEN your abdominal muscles to hold your back in place.

L: Lift with your LEGS (never pick up by bending at the waist).

B: BREATHE through each move. Avoid holding your breath and making that "huuunh!" sound. You want to get oxygen to your blood, which will deliver it to your muscles.

And now that you have a filthy mnemonic (the BEST KIND) to give you some general safety guidelines, let's look at those workouts to get you started! We'll give you some inaugural exercises in the three different types of locations you might find yourself. If you're an aquatic-based life form, like a mollusk or a Merman, then (a) I can't help you and (b) how are you reading this book under water?

KEY THINGS TO KEEP IN YOUR NOODLE

➤ Drink plenty of water.
➤ Stretch before and after.
➤ Be patient and move slowly.
➤ If you feel pain, overheating, or shortness of breath: STOP.
➤ Consult a physician or professional fitness trainer if you have questions, injuries, or concerns.

Make sure to record your workouts in your Character Tome. And give yourself 10 XP each time you complete one!

WORKOUT 1: GYM

Chest

Now that you're a secure, confident human you're going to be leading with your chest wherever you go. Naturally, you'll probably want to target this area for improvement to achieve what scientists refer to as "lusciously fuckable" pecs. Here are some basics:

- The chest is worked by pushing weights away from it.
- You may lie on a weight bench and use a dumbbell in each hand or a straight bar with weights on it (using a spotter is highly recommended).
- You may also use machine equipment, which can be easier and force you into proper form a bit better.
- As a general rule with weights, give a slight pause at the moment of muscle contraction.

FREE WEIGHTS: FLAT BENCH BARBELL PRESS

- Lie down on a flat bench with a straight bar.
- Keep your back flat on the bench and feet planted on the floor.
- Push the weights away from your chest.
- Exhale on the pushing/upward motion.
- DO 2 SETS OF 15–20 REPS.

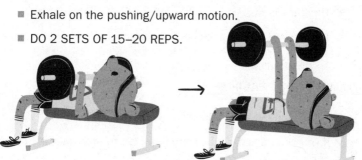

MACHINE: CHEST PRESS (OR FLYS)

- Seat yourself on a "Pec Dec" or fly machine. (Usually these machines have instructions on the side for further help.)

- Keep your back straight and feet on the floor.

- Exhale on the pushing/outward motion.

- DO 2 SETS OF 15–20 REPS.

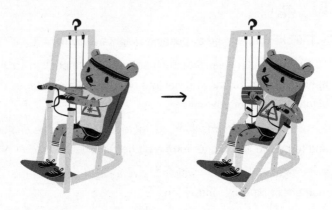

Back

Hooray! You've worked your chest! Now you gotta work the other side of the house to support the front.

- The back is worked by pulling into or TOWARD the body.

- Tom suggests two machines for your back:

MACHINE: LATERAL PULL-DOWNS

- This is a seated machine with a cable.

- If you can't figure out how much weight to start with, try half your body weight.

■ Grab the bar, and sit down on the bench while scooting your legs under the pads.

■ Keep your back straight.

■ Perform the exercise by pulling the cable down toward your chest (not behind the head) while keeping your forearms perpendicular to the ground.

■ Pull with your upper back muscles (latissimus dorsi) more than your arms.

■ Exhale as you pull.

■ DO 2 SETS OF 15–20 REPS.

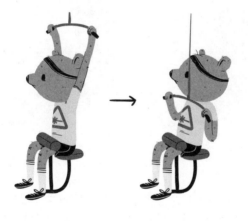

MACHINE: SEATED ROWS

- This mimics the motion of rowing, as you may have guessed from the title.

- Sit down and place your feet on the apparatus in front of you.

- Grab the handlebar and pull straight into your body.

- Keep your back straight and your neck in line with your spine.

- Exhale while you pull.

- DO 2 SETS OF 15–20 REPS

Shoulders

As long as we're hitting the chest and the back, let's pack some shoulder steaks onto that ever-improving body of yours! Most people obsess over arms or abs, but it's the SHOULDERS that give a human that fit, V shape.

- To work the shoulders you can be either standing or seated, but let's seat you to reduce chance of poor form and injury.

MACHINE: SHOULDER PRESS

- Select a weight that isn't too heavy but gives you a little resistance.

■ Sit away from the machine with your back straight against the cushion and your feet planted firmly on the ground directly under your knees.

■ Set the handles a few inches above your shoulders.

■ Now reach up and hold the handles on either side of your head.

■ Extend your arms upward while exhaling but don't lock your elbows at the top.

■ Lower the weight but don't allow the weight stack to descend fully.

■ Keep the up-and-down motion slow and fluid.

■ DO 2 SETS OF 15–20 REPS.

MACHINE: LATERAL RAISES

■ Go extra-light on the weight; these are harder than they look and this probably isn't a muscle group you use regularly.

■ Sit away from the machine with your back straight against the cushion and your feet planted firmly on the ground directly under your knees.

■ The pads will be on the outsides of your arms.

- Adjust the seat height so that your arms comfortably follow the pads up to your grip on the handles.

- Now push your elbows upward until they are about ear level, hold for a second, and lower them back down.

- You might look like you are flapping wings, but please refrain from squawking if in a crowded gym.

- DO 2 SETS OF 10 REPS.

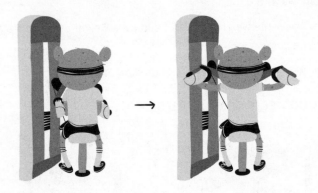

Biceps

There is no muscle more synonymous with "tough guy" than the bicep. You don't have to be a tough guy nor do you need large biceps for people to like you. With just a little work, though, you can tone yours to the point where people will subconsciously notice them in a short-sleeve shirt and take you for a person who likes himself enough to take care of himself. This is attractive to potential mates and/or orgasm inducers.

MACHINE: PREACHER CURLS

I can only assume that part of the reason they call them "preacher curls" is because you will exclaim "sweet Jesus!" the day after doing them. The advantage to this machine is that it basically forces you into good form. GREAT for a beginner.

- Sit down and rest your arms over the padded decline bench.

- Adjust the seat so that the pad comes close to your armpits.

- Keep your elbows shoulder-width apart, and make sure to keep them still and planted on the padding.

- Now curl the weight toward your body until your arms are just past vertical.

- Pause on top and squeeze, then slowly lower back down.

- DO 2 SETS OF 15 REPS.

MACHINE: CABLE CURLS

A "cable curl" SOUNDS like a dangerous sexual act, but it is a good way to isolate the biceps for maximum efficiency.

- Attach the W-shaped bar to the cable machine.

- Keep the weight low, as these will get hard FAST.

- Bend your knees slightly, and step one leg back to offer more stability.

- Keep your back straight and your shoulders back (you should only feel this in your biceps).

- DO NOT swing your body or shoulders to complete a rep.

- Pull the handle up to your chest while exhaling.

- Slowly and smoothly drop the bar back down without fully extending your arms.

- DO NOT let the weight drop.

- DO 2 SETS OF 15 REPS.

Triceps

Rounding out those spindly nose-wipers you call arms are the triceps brachii—or "three-headed arm muscle," which I far prefer calling it—which connects your elbow to your shoulder, allowing for a greater flourish when flipping people off.

MACHINE: TRICEPS CABLE ROPE EXTENSIONS

- The rope will have two equal segments forming a V-shape with little nubs at each end.

- Stand facing the machine and grab each side of the rope.

- Keep your back straight and your knees bent slightly.

- Start with your arms about navel height.

- Keeping your elbows still, pull down until you reach your full range of motion.

- Pause for a second and contract your triceps.

- Slowly raise your forearms back to starting position.

- Exhale on the downward motion.

- DO 2 SETS OF 15 REPS.

MACHINE: TRICEPS EXTENSIONS

This exercise looks similar to the preacher curls, only instead of pulling upward you're going to be pushing down to work the other side of your arms.

- Start with a light weight, as these get difficult quickly.

- Sit down and grasp the handles.

- Place your forearms on the armrest.

- Keep you feet planted on the floor and your back against the seat.

- Slowly push down with your forearms. You should only feel your triceps doing the work.

- Pause at the bottom and contract.

- Slowly return your arms to starting position.

- Exhale on the downward motion.

- If your body is squirmy or flailing while you're doing these, lower the weight.

- DO 2 SETS OF 15 REPS.

Legs

Those two trunky things that split off at your pink parts can turn into useless string cheese if you sit at a computer all day and night. To work the upper legs (quads and hammies), there are two main exercises you'll want to explore: squats and lunges. There are a couple of different squat machines: On one you will be raising your body and weights, and the other you'll be pushing weights away from you, so feel free to pick the one that whispers your name when you stare at it for too long, but don't do both on the same day. Both are good for beginners because your positioning in the machine reduces your risk for injury. Hoorays!

MACHINE: HACK SQUATS

This machine will be at a 45-degree angle and strengthens your legs by creating resistance when you push your body upward from a squatting position. Hack Squats is a silly-sounding name. I would have called them Fart Sits.

- Load equal weights on both sides of the machine.

- Step onto the platform with your feet slightly wider than your shoulders.

- Put your back flat against the back pad and rest your shoulders under the shoulder pads (seems logical).

- There's a locking mechanism on the machine, so extend your legs to open the full range of motion.

- Slowly squat down until your thighs are parallel with the platform.

- Push yourself back up to starting position but don't go so high that you lock your knees.

- When you're done, push back up to relock the machine into position before trying to get out.

- DO 2 SETS OF 15 REPS.

MACHINE: LEG PRESSES

With these guys, you'll be seated in the closest thing a gym has to a recliner. The idea is to push a weighted platform away from your body with your gams.

- Set your weights on the post.

- Sit down and make sure your back and butt are resting against the seat as far back as you can go.

- Place your whole feet on the platform slightly farther than shoulder-width apart.

- Grab the handles on either side of the bench for support.

- Slowly extend your legs without fully extending them or locking your knees.

- Slowly go back to starting position.

- DO 2 SETS OF 15 REPS.

Abs

CRUNCHES

Don't confuse crunches with sit-ups! They're not quite the same thing. Also the name "crunch" is gross, IMHO.

- Lie on the floor.

- Put your hands behind your head (sometimes I Superman my arms forward).

- Bend your knees so that your feet are planted and pulled closer to your body.

- Contract your ab muscles while keeping your neck in line with your back.

- You should only lift your back off the ground a little bit.

- DO 3 SETS OF 25 REPS.

FINITO! Now do a cooldown stretch! (See "Stretching.")

WORKOUT 2: HOME

If you don't want to drop the cash every month to belong to a gym, that's fine. It requires a tad more discipline, but you can get some stellar workouts in your own dwelling. Many people think you need fancy equipment to *really* train, but you don't. You can have just as diverse a workout regime by switching up things like hand position, exercise order, number of sets, number of reps, and weights used. Tom has kept me in shape using only a yoga mat, four dumbbell sets (ten, fifteen, twenty, and twenty-five pounds), an exercise ball, and a pull-up bar. NOTE: A pull-up bar isn't required, but it's GREAT if you can install one.

Chest

The easiest way to work the chest, especially if you are not at a gym, is the push-up. No matter how many scientific breakthrough fitness devices we see on late-night infomercials, there's still nothing better than a person, the ground, and the resistance of gravity. Now to modify it with a breakthrough fitness device: the exercise ball. If you're going to invest $40 in a piece of equipment to keep at the house/apartment/basement/floating castle, this is a good one. The ball can be used for stretching, ab exercises, balance/core training, sitting at the computer to keep you from slouching, and modified push-ups.

PUSH-UPS ON THE BALL

■ Place your palms on the ball apart from each other with your hands pointed outward; I can't tell you exactly where as this is a balancing thing that will vary slightly for every person.

■ Get into push-up position and begin.

■ Your arms may feel a little wobbly, so go SLOWLY.

■ This balancing act will also strengthen your core.

■ TRY 10 REPS, AND IF THOSE ARE EASY, GO TO 20 REPS.

CHEST PRESSES ON THE BALL

■ Start seated on the ball and slowly walk your feet out until your neck and shoulders are resting on the ball.

■ Your body should be parallel to the floor and your feet directly under your knees.

■ Hold your body firm; don't let it droop.

■ Use your appropriately selected dumbbell weight.

- Push the weights up and away from your chest, like a bench press.

- DO 2 SETS OF 10 REPS.

Back

LOWER BACK EXTENSIONS

- Squat in front of your exercise ball.

- Facing down, fold your body over the ball so that your midsection is around the equator of the ball.

- Your knees will almost touch the floor on one side and your face on the other (depending on how tall you are).

- I rest my tiptoes on the floor and my heels against the wall for support.

- Now put your hands behind your head like you're on *Cops*.

- Using your back, lift your upper body until you're parallel with the ground.

- Slowly fold back down.

- DO 2 SETS OF 15 REPS.

DUMBBELL ROWS

■ Standing up, bend over like a downhill skier, your torso not quite parallel with the ground.

■ Keep your knees bent.

■ Hold a dumbbell in each hand and start with your arms hanging, elbows bent slightly.

■ Raise your elbows back toward the ceiling, contracting your upper back to pull them up. Think of it like you're trying to pull your shoulder blades closer together.

■ Alternate between keeping your elbows close to your body for narrow pulls and bringing them out perpendicular to your body for wide pulls.

■ DO 2 SETS OF 15 REPS.

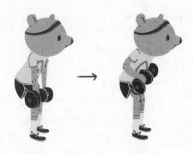

Shoulders

SEATED MILITARY PRESSES

- Sit on the exercise ball.

- Keep your back straight, your eyes forward, and your knees over your feet.

- With a dumbbell in each hand, hold your wrists over your elbows in the air in an "I give up!" pose.

- Raise the dumbbells over your head, coming in slightly toward each other on top.

- Lower back to starting position.

- DO 2 SETS OF 15 REPS.

DUMBBELL LATERAL RAISES

- You can do these seated on a ball or standing. If standing up, bend at the knees slightly to remove pressure from your back.

- Keep your back straight and your eyes forward.

- Start with the dumbbells in your hands resting at your sides.

- Lift both arms perpendicular to your body until they are parallel with the ground.

- Keep your elbows slightly bent.

- Now go like this: "A-WOOOOO-gah!"

- Lower back to starting position.

- DO 2 SETS OF 15 REPS.

Biceps

Biceps! One of our most unused muscles. Shoving multiple hot dogs into your food hole doesn't count as "curling." Fortunately, they are easy to work out and will build quickly. You can increase the effectiveness of the exercise by changing hand position and switching from doing both arms at the same time to alternating in a left arm, then right arm, then left arm, then right arm fashion.

DUMBBELL CURLS

- You can do these standing or seated on the ball.

- If standing, bend your knees slightly and keep your upper body straight and locked.

- If seated, keep your back straight and your feet shoulder-width apart and under your knees.

- The motion should be isolated to your biceps; don't flail to complete reps.

- Do one set with your palms facing forward, then try another set with your palms facing away from your body; this will target different parts of the biceps.

- DO 2 SETS OF 15 REPS.

Triceps

The main thing to remember is to keep the elbows STILL. You should only feel your triceps while performing these.

DUMBBELL TRICEPS KICKBACKS

- Just like the dumbbell rows for the back, assume the downhill skier position.

- Your lower back should stay flat (in other words, keep your spine in one straight line).

- With your elbows bent and arms tightly at your sides, extend your arms backward.

- Pause while extended and contract the triceps while exhaling.

- DO 2 SETS OF 15–20 REPS.

SEATED ONE-ARM TRICEPS EXTENSIONS

■ Sit down on your ball (tee-hee).

■ Keep your back straight and your eyes forward.

■ Rest one arm across your body until your hand is touching your opposite hip.

■ Lift the dumbbell in your other arm over your head and bend it at a 90-degree angle as if you were trying to scratch your back.

■ Now straighten your arm while exhaling and contracting the triceps.

■ Lower back to the starting position.

■ DO 2 SETS OF 15–20 REPS.

Legs

That's right, it's your old pals Squats and Lunges! This time you won't need any snazzy equipment, just the right form. A nice option for reducing stress on your knees is to perform squats with an exercise ball pinned between your back and the wall. The ball will move up and down with you, also giving you constant lower back support. The rubbery ball mashed up against you feels oddly satisfying, too.

FREESTANDING SQUATS

- Stand with your feet slightly wider than your shoulders.

- Hold your arms straight ahead or place them on your hips.

- Keep your back straight, your eyes forward, and your knees slightly bent.

- In your downward motion, you'll be sitting into a squat position until your thighs are parallel to the ground.

- Focus on keeping your weight back on your heels.

- Stand back up, but don't fully extend your legs or lock your knees.

- Keep the motion slow and fluid.

- DO 2 SETS OF 15 REPS.

STATIONARY LUNGES

- Stand with your feet about six inches apart.

- Place one leg forward and step the other back until you're up on the ball of your foot (or "your feet's balls" as I childishly call them).

- Place your hands on your hips.

- Keep your back straight and your eyes forward.

- Lunge downward but don't let your back knee hit the floor.

- Make sure your front knee doesn't drift out past your toes on the downward motion.

- Stand back up but don't fully extend your legs or lock your front knee.

- Keep the motion slow and fluid.

- DO 2 SETS OF 15 REPS.

AB CRUNCHES ON THE BALL

I do these with my knees bent and my feet resting up against the baseboard of the wall for stability.

- Place your butt at a 45-degree angle from the center of the exercise ball.

■ Place your hands behind your head.

■ Crunch upward, contracting your abdominal muscles to pull you up. Be careful not to arch your back.

■ Let your body fold back against the curve of the ball on the downward motion.

■ DO 3 SETS OF 25 REPS.

Stretch!

WORKOUT 3: ON THE ROAD

This may not apply to you, but as I travel with the frequency of a junior flight attendant, it's important for me to have options for exercising in hotels. Tom has always stressed to me that—away from the comfort and familiarity of my regular exercise equipment and routine—my goal is to continue working out, not to get into better shape while I'm gone. In other words, think of these as maintenance workouts to keep your blood flowing until you can get back home. These will be light, conservative workouts that will help you avoid injury. I learned this lesson in an unpleasant way: I was in New York a few years back, and I went down to the hotel gym for a run on the treadmill. I got this thing in my head that I was going to run as hard as I could for thirty minutes, just to be able to report back to Tom how awesome I was. I completed the run, but because it was new to me, I hadn't thought to stretch well enough before or after. Even if I had, it wouldn't have helped. My lower back told me to fuck off almost immediately after, and I was bedridden in a pain cloud for several days. It took a few weeks to resume my normal workout level. My attempt to leap forward in one day led to a giant step back. Try to avoid the ego-driven workouts when you're alone.

When we travel, our patterns are broken and we tend to work out less, eat worse, and drink more. We get the "Eh, fuckit!" attitude. This is fine as long as you understand that it will be a little more work getting back to where you were when you return home. CONSISTENCY is your new friend. No matter how "small" and "pointless" you think a little exercise is— honestly, fifteen to twenty minutes of yoga, stretching, or walking in the morning is enough on the road—just train yourself to do it. Philosophically, a workout is not always blasting heavy weights, burning the most calories you can, or achieving some new height in your fitness level. A workout can be as simple as stretching, if that is what your body needs.

The ultimate goal involves getting to a place in your fitness where you can have a dialogue with your body (instead of just listening to it bitch at you). The more I worked out, the more I understood what I needed at any given time. Learning to listen to my body over my ego has helped me maintain a level of pain-free fitness these last few years. This should be your ultimate fitness goal.

With all that in mind, here are some small yet effective items you bring with you on your travels:

- A yoga mat
- A small foam roller
- Resistance bands or exercise tubing

With just those few items you will be able to maintain a workout regime and avoid the normal stress and tension caused by traveling, not having your gym, and not sleeping in your own bed (all of which can make your body turn on you). Full disclosure: I don't travel with any of this, but I still think they're good suggestions. I tend to focus on cardio and stretching, as most hotels have gyms in our modern era. It really just depends on what you like and are comfortable with. I saw a woman in the San Francisco airport pull out her mat, partially disrobe, and drop a steaming pile of yoga right there at the gate. A guy next to her decided that her routine needed to be set to guitar riffs. I decided to join in with something I was good at, too, so I tweeted the whole thing.

"Fine. You're going to do yoga? I'll practice 'Blackbird' loudly."

This display was a bit much to me, like, "Hey, everyone! I do yoga! See??" But who the hell am I to judge? I hosted *Shipmates*.

Chest

Once again the easiest, anytime/anywhere snack: push-ups. Make sure to keep your back flat and your neck in line with your spine. One way to vary the push-up move is to change your hand position. You can also modify the push-up by doing it with bent knees.

PUSH-UPS: FIRST SET

■ Place your hands on the floor wider than shoulder width and assume the push-up position. Rest knees on the ground if you want to reduce the level of difficulty.

■ DO 10–15 REPS.

PUSH-UPS: SECOND SET

■ Use a narrower hand position, like shoulder-width apart while keeping your elbows tight against your body, and assume the push-up position.

■ If you really want to try some ninja shit, put your hands on the floor such that your thumbs and index fingers touch to form a triangle and do push-ups from there.

■ DO 10–15 REPS.

What? Bored ALREADY? OK! Try these!

INCLINE/DECLINE PUSH-UPS

■ Put your feet on a chair (often found in even the fleabaggiest hotel rooms) and your hands on the floor and do the push-ups.

■ OR put your hands on the chair and your feet on the floor and GO.

■ DO 10–15 REPS OF EITHER.

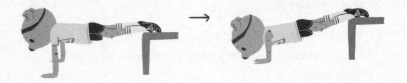

Back

Resistance band time! You can buy one on the webs for $10.
The main exercise motion for the back involves pulling toward
your body, so this will give you a perfect amount of resistance,
as the title so deftly denotes. Many of these will come with a
clip or attachment that you can connect to a door, which will be
the stationary object from which you will be pulling.

NARROW BACK PULLS

■ Attach the hook or clip at the middle of the band to a door or
other stable, stationary object. Grasp the handles in each hand.

■ Stand just far enough away that the band is taut.

■ Stand with your back straight and your knees slightly bent.

■ Move one leg forward and step one back slightly to give you
some stability.

■ Start with your arms in front of you, palms down.

■ Pull back until your elbows are tight at your sides while
rotating your hands 90 degrees. Your palms should end up
facing each other.

■ Use a slow, controlled movement to get back to the starting
position.

■ Exhale on the pull.

■ DO 2 SETS OF 15 REPS.

WIDE BACK PULLS

- Same as above, but keep your palms down and pull straight back with your elbows perpendicular to your body.
- DO 2 SETS OF 15 REPS.

Two Variations to Toggle Difficulty:

- Do one arm at a time!
- Do them on one leg!
  - » Stand with one leg slightly bent.
  - » Bring your other knee up until your thigh is perpendicular to your body.
  - » Don't lean back or raise your shoulders.
  - » Switch legs between sets.

Shoulders

What's that? You want MORE band exercises?! Well, OK! Your happiness is my food, after all! Instead of forcing a door to help you, this time you will stand on the midpoint of the tubing while grasping the handles. Your feet will help create more tension: one for less, both for more. To add further resistance, spread your feet apart but no more than shoulder width.

LATERAL RAISES

- Stand with your hands at your sides.

- Keep your arms straightish (never lock anything).

- Keep your knees slightly bent and your back straight.

- Raise your arms outward until they are parallel to the ground. Think of the doors opening on your DeLorean time machine when you get in it to go back and show your old self how incredimazeballs you're going to look in the future.

- Lower your arms to the starting position.

- DO 2 SETS OF 15 REPS.

FRONT RAISES

- Same as lateral raises EXCEPT you will raise your arms straight ahead and upward until they are parallel to the floor.
- DO 2 SETS OF 15 REPS.

Biceps

The biceps curl motion is pretty basic, so the trick to getting the best results is to again alternate the positioning of your arms. Your muscles are not flat, as the Church once believed. They are three-dimensional! Changing positions targets the muscle groups more fully, which is what people refer to when they use the term "body sculpting." Slightly annoying people, I'd say. The same ones who also say "anyhoo" and "jazz fusion."

STANDING BAND CURLS

- Stand on the band in whichever resistance configuration works best for you.
- Knees slightly bent! Back straight! Eyes forward! (Are you sensing a pattern?)
- Hold your arms at your side with the palms facing forward.
- Keeping your body still, do the curling motion.

- DO 1 SET OF 15 REPS.

- For the second set, point your forearms at 45-degree angles from your body (well, technically one arm is 45 degrees and the other is 135 degrees, but let's not get too mathy.)

- Curl up and in toward your body.

- DO 1 SET OF 15 REPS.

ALTERNATING BAND CURLS

- Now do the same two exercises above, but this time alternate your arms one at a time instead of curling both simultaneously!

- DO 1 SET OF 15 REPS FOR EACH ARM.

Triceps

Only one of the following two exercises will use the band this time.

BAND TRICEPS EXTENSIONS

■ Attach the hook or clip at the middle of the band to a door or other stable, stationary object. You can also sit on the band to keep it from flying back and smashing in your face meat.

■ Face said stationary object.

■ Assume the downhill skier position (lower back flat and not arched, neck in line with spine, knees slightly bent).

■ Extend your arms back at the elbow, keeping them tight to your body.

■ Exhale on the extension. (As a general rule, you want to exhale TOWARD the muscle contraction and inhale AWAY from it.)

■ DO 2 SETS OF 15–20 REPS.

TRICEPS BENCH EXTENSIONS (DIPS)

■ Get a chair or other object that comes up about as high as the seat. (I've used the edge of a bathtub.)

- Make SURE it is stable, otherwise it could tip forward and you will fall and cry.

- Place your hands on the edge and lightly grasp the lip of the object.

- Extend your feet together on the ground out in front of you.

- Holding your upper body up with your arms, dip down slowly until your elbows create a 90-degree angle.

- Push yourself back up.

- DO 2 SETS OF 15–20 REPS.

Legs

You guessed it! Squats and lunges! You need exactly zero equipment for these.

FREESTANDING SQUATS

- Place your feet slightly farther apart than shoulder width.

- Keep your lower back straight.

- Hold your hands straight out in front of you, straight to your sides, or on your hips (the latter being the easiest).

- Bend your knees and drop your butt bulbs toward your heels until you are squatting while being mindful not to crap on the floor.

- Make sure your knees don't go out over your toes on the bend, as this will put undue stress on your knees.
  - » It is FAR better to go only halfway down than to push too far forward.
  - » NEVER put stress on one area of your body while targeting another.
  - » ALWAYS err on the side of caution.
  - » Outline subheadings are COOL.
- DO 2 SETS OF 15–20 REPS.

STATIONARY LUNGES

- Stand with one leg in front and the other leg back and up onto your foot's balls.

- Keep your back straight, your eyes forward, and your hands on your hips.

- Lower into a lunge, but don't let your front knee go past your damn toes!!!

- DO 2 SETS OF 15–20 REPS (swap leg positions between sets).

IMPORTANT POINTS!

- Posture and proper alignment are most important to ensure good technique and best results.

- Overtraining without enough recovery time will lead to injury. :(← frowny

- Vary order and type of cardio, weight resistance, and interval training to shock your muscles.

- Go slowly and always check in with your body.

- STRETCH.

NUTRITIONY BUSINESS!

I'm not going to go SUPER in-depth on nutrition, because there are books written by professionals that will do exactly that. If you're Gwyneth Paltrow, you would just hire nine kinds of nutritionists. Also, if you're Gwyneth Paltrow and you're reading my book, YOU ARE A SUPERLATIVE MILF. If you had a walrus moustache, you'd be Milford Brimley.

Instead of really specific dietary instructions and recipes, here are the nutrition highlights that Trainer Tom shared with me when I first asked, "What should I be putting into my food hole?" so many years ago. He provided the bullet points, I added the explanations:

(Yet another DISCLAIMER: Do at your own risk; please don't sue me; I think you're nice; bladdity bloo.)

nUTRITIOn HIGHLIGHTS

- **Eat four or five small meals a day.**

Eating throughout the day keeps your metabolism running smoothly. Think of your body like an old choo choo. Some poor son of a bitch (a stoker) had to shovel coal into the firebox to heat the water tubes to produce steam. If he shoveled too little, the water would cool and the train would slow down and eventually stop. If he shoveled too much, he could smother the fire to the same result. Steady, consistent fueling keeps a train going! You're the train, and food is the coal. And since we're being other things, I'm a bird! A pretty, pretty bird!

- **Go no longer than three or four hours between meals.**

It's not only important to eat throughout the day to keep your metabolism going, but if you wait too long to eat you are going to want to stuff as much bad junk into your drooling mouth as possible. Your body's fuel supply is down, and it's looking to stoke it as quickly as possible, and it reasons that pizza will do that as quickly as possible. If you're eating right, you won't really have cravings for healthy food. In fact, if you do crave something over and over again, you might actually be allergic to it. WTF, Body??

- **Water, water, and water.**

While there's no exact answer as to how much you should drink, the Mayo Clinic suggests the "8 x 8 rule" for regular folks: 8 ounces of water 8 times a day. A good thing to keep in mind for me was to make water my main drink, my go-to. Keep an eye on your pee (but not IN your pee). Healthy pee should be relatively clear. Bright yellow pee means you need more water (unless you are taking vitamins, in which case, your pee looks electric).

Don't make yourself sick drinking water, as overhydration, or water toxicity, really is dangerous. Look that shit up if you don't believe me!

- **Reduce or eliminate salt and sugar.**

Salt (NaCl, sodium chloride) makes you retain water. If you feel like you're looking particularly bloaty, you are either a sentient walrus or consuming too much salt. When you're choosing what to eat, think logically about what purpose the dominant ingredient will serve in your body. Eating sugary stuff will fill you up, but the calories are empty. In other words, they have no redeeming nutrient value and will do little more than just cling to fat, like little adipose monkeys. This will slow down fat burning, which is the OPPOSITE of what you want.

- **Reduce or eliminate complex/starchy carbs.**

The word "carbs" is as bad as the word "fuck" to some people, particularly in our weird half-assed-version-of-the-Atkin's-Diet-obsessed society. In truth, carbs are the fuel that your body needs to exert energy. This is very simple:

CARBS = ENERGY & PROTEIN = MUSCLE

If you have trouble remembering this four-word formula, just use another delightful mnemonic: Can Everyone Pee More? C-E P-M (Carbs-Energy Protein-Muscle).

The KIND of carbs you ingest is another matter. White rice, bread, pasta, and potatoes are all assholes you should try to avoid. If you have to eat one of those, rice is the most acceptable, but brown rice even more so. Remember that unburned carbs will be stored as fat, so try to eat those before 4 p.m. (if you go to bed at a reasonable hour) so that your body has time to burn them off. Friendly carbs, according to goodcarbs.org, "are unprocessed carbohydrates in their natural state—or *very close* to their natural state." Green vegetables, leafy vegetables, beans, legumes (peas, beans, pod fruit—"legume" is a dumb-sounding word that comes from the Latin *legere*, to gather; as in, these foods were commonly "gathered" by our ancestors). Years ago, I tried an all-protein diet. I felt lethargic and my stomach hurt. This was remedied when I started eating good carbs along with the protein. If you are GOING to eat starchy carbs, then do it earlier in the day so you have a better chance of metabolizing them. And make sure to eat water-rich foods like vegetables later in the day for shitsake!

- **We must all take in "good fat" (there is a difference).**
GOOD FAT: Monounsaturated—nuts, avocado, olive oil
BAD FAT: Saturated—coconut oil, palm oil

GOOD FAT: Polyunsaturated—salmon, fish oil, safflower, omega-3s
BAD FAT: Trans—hydrogenated, packaged foods, fast food, vegetable shortening

GOOD FAT: Albert
BAD FAT: Jabba the Hutt

- **Keep caloric intake up.**

While it's true that to lose pounds it's better to cut your caloric intake than just your bad fat intake, but eating better doesn't mean starving yourself. When your body goes into hunger mode, it is inclined to store fat. To the protohumans, hunger meant delicious tubers were scarce and the body needed to hold on to as many nutrients as possible until more could be found. Truthfully, if you're eating properly you should never feel hungry. If you feel sick to your stomach and zombielike, you're not eating enough of the right foods. ESPECIALLY if you work out. In this case, you're attempting to burn even more so you have to keep the fire extra stoked. Eventually, going on a hunger strike diet will take off weight, but it will also take off valuable things like muscle, good fat, and your will to live.

- **You truly "are what you eat."**

Here's a good basic rule of thumb: look at your food's physical attributes. Bread, cake, and pasta are doughy, fluffy, and squishy and they will express themselves on your person thusly. Fortunately, fish, chicken breasts, and apples are lean and firm with tight skin. These are more of the qualities you might be seeking. They look healthy because they ARE, and they will pass those savings onto YOU, the Consumer!!!

- **One glass of alcohol → one glass of water.**

For every boozy drink you have, have a water. If I had done this while I was drinking, I might have died from overhydration. If you drink like a normal person, this shouldn't be a problem.

- **Try to take in protein, carbs, and fat at at least two meals a day.**

Protein builds muscle! It also boosts your metabolism, which in turn will burn fat. As you eat healthier your body will go after the protein, so make sure to keep up your intake. So what's a good number of grams per day of protein? Ideally men want 1.5 grams of protein per kilo of body weight, knowing that 1 kilogram = 2.2 pounds. Women want 1 gram of protein per kilo of body weight. Math Nerds, assemble!

Your weight in pounds / 2.2 = your weight in kilograms
Your weight in kilograms x 1.5 = ideal daily protein intake in grams

. . . so with actual numbers that would look like this:

200 pounds / 2.2 = 90.9 kilograms
90.9 x 1.5 = ~136 grams of protein

Special note! Don't eat all of your protein in one sitting and go, "I'm DOING it!!!" Spread it out as evenly as possible over five or six smaller meals, which would put you in the 20 to 30 grams-of-protein-per-meal range. Remember! This is a guideline, so if you don't eat EXACTLY what you've calculated every day, it's OK. This should just give you an idea of where to aim. There are a comical number of apps for your smartdevices that will keep track of your daily protein/calorie/sodium/whatever-you-care-about intake. I used one out of curiosity for just a week and discovered that I was only eating about half the protein every day that I actually needed (and WAY too much sodium). *The more you know. . . .* [inspirational star cascades over the cold vacuum of space]

- **The most important thing is CONSISTENCY.**

Rather than just committing to work out and eat better, commit to the concept of consistency. It sounds strange, but this slight goal adjustment might help you have better results when you find yourself trying to justify eating a whole pie by yourself.

- **Supplements: multivitamins, vitamin B3 for men, and iron and calcium for women.**

Men don't need as much iron as ladies. This is because we don't menstruate very often. Oh sure, it SOUNDS rad, but most dudes are just too damn lazy to produce eggs and then slough them through the penis. The calcium is helpful to women because they are more susceptible to bone density loss and the B3 (also called niacin) for men because it gives dudes the energy to support their typically higher muscle mass. Or you could just hedge all your bets and take a sex-specific multivitamin. I use 365's "Adult Multi for Men," which I purchase at Whole Foods, who are not paying me to say that but SHOULD.

- **The two most important meals are breakfast and post-workout.**

Skipping breakfast slows down your metabolism. Also, when you're REALLY hungry later in the day, you're liable to nuke your body with carbs. When exercising, eating thirty minutes to two hours after a workout replaces glycogen and encourages the rebuilding of the muscle fiber you just tore down. Eat good carbs AND protein. If solid food is difficult after exercise, a protein drink will work.

- **Use portion control.**

Say, if you eat smaller portions, YOU'LL HAVE LESS FOOD TO PROCESS, which will keep you from gaining weight or help you lose the chubs you have. It is better for you to eat the same daily calories over more meals then fewer with larger portions. For some reason, we have equated "eating until really full" with "awesome." This is a goddamn lie. The food's going down, but your brain needs to receive the signal that you shoved it in. After about twenty minutes, you should no longer be hungry (eating s-l-o-w-l-y should help manage this as well). I personally cut my portion sizes in half when I was a tugboat, which kept me from getting full and trimmed me down.

- **Do not eat two to three hours before bed.**

For reals! Your food may not digest properly if you take a pizza to bed. (I don't mean "have sex with." That I'm actually OK with.) This may leave you bloated and crampy the next morning. Also, your body needs all the energy it can get to repair your body while you sleep. If you give it a friggin' job, like digesting your food, you not only will sleep poorly but the double duty your body is pulling will force it to store whatever it couldn't break down as fat. The upside is that your extra layer of goo will save you money on blankets.

FITNESS HIGHLIGHTS

- The most important thing about working out is consistency!!!
- The most important thing about fitness is contraction, using lighter weights to pump maximum blood into your muscles.
- Work the full rotation of muscle: power-lifting mentality (full range of muscle) vs. bodybuilding mentality.
- Do not grow in the gym; growth takes place with rest and proper nutrition.
- Posture and proper alignment are most important for preventing injury.

- The first five minutes of cardio flushes out stored carbs in the body.
- Better diet = less cardio.
- Depletion of calories will burn lean muscle mass.
- Overtraining, breaking down muscles, and not allowing enough recovery time will lead to injury.
- The most important supplement is food!!
- Minimum cardio: Reach THR (target heart rate) a minimum of three times a week. Your THR should be 60–70% for fat burn, 70–80% for cardiovascular.
- For the sake of stress on your joints, it's better to walk at a good pace at an incline than to run.
- For stamina and endurance, include interval training (to elevate your heart rate).
- Vary the type of cardio, weight resistance, and interval training to shock your muscles.
- If under the age of seventeen, be careful of growth areas, i.e., spine, shoulders, and knees.
- At any age, core strength is most important! Build solid core strength, then pursue weight strength and muscle size. Endurance builds strength!
- Check your ego!

A SUMMARIZED PRIORITY LIST FOR LIST WHORES

1. CONSISTENCY: Commit to doing the best you can every day!
2. PORTION CONTROL: Don't eat until you get full.
3. A CHEAT DAY: Seriously, ANYTHING you want.
4. HEALTHY SNACKS: Almonds, fruit, yogurt, string cheese.
5. WATER: Make water your go-to beverage!

6. DO NOT EAT TWO HOURS BEFORE BED: Can't really expand on that one.

7. DON'T PUNCH PEOPLE IN THE FACE: I mean, as long as we're making lists . . .

CHECK THAT BOX!

In the lifelong pursuit of fitness and feeling better, you will ALWAYS get an "A" for effort. For the first couple of years of my manly workouts, I avoided exercising while traveling because I just wasn't sure what I was supposed to do, and the pain of ignorance far outweighed the desire to have a luscious body (wait . . . WHAAAA??). Then while doing a series of stand-up gigs at colleges in central Illinois (I was following the path of the great Lincoln-Douglas debates: "This declared indifference, but, as I must think, covert real zeal for the spread of slavery, I cannot but hate." Abe FTW!) Anyway, it was during the winter and I believe the National Weather Service had declared the area "Hoth," so I was left with a day of nothing to do in a Hampton Inn in a small town. (Hampton has the best beds in a pinch and are in all small towns. No, they are not paying me but certainly SHOULD.) "Say . . . maybe I'll see if there's a fitness room . . . that should crush some of this boredom!" Let it be noted that the broadband in the hotel leaked out of the Ethernet cable like tree sap, so anything more than email was unrealistic. Yes! There was a fitness room. Most hotels have them now. In this case, it was just a treadmill and an exercise bike, but it was enough. I stretched for five minutes and ran for twenty. That was all. I felt better.

When I got back to Apartment Dojo, I shamefully recanted my minuscule workout.

"Bro!" said Trainer Tom. "That's GREAT!"

"It is? But I only jogged on the treadmill for, like, twenty minutes."

And this is the following sentence that shifted my worldview of consistent exercise and made it seem plausible: *"It doesn't matter what you do . . . as long as you check that 'Did I work out today' box with a yes!"*

And it suddenly made a bunch of sense. Two years prior, I was in terrible shape, and now here I was CHOOSING to exercise without someone standing over me telling me what to do. The benefits are twofold: (1) Some exercise is better than NO exercise. Always. (2) Something joyful surges in your brain when you make what Tom calls "pro-you" decisions. You're saying to yourself, "Hey, Self, you're not such a douchey assclown after all!" and that internal sentiment will have positive, penetrative ramifications on your psyche for the rest of the day. When I can work out with Tom (or a workout compatriot), I'll hit it a little harder but when I'm on the road or only left with a little bit of time, I make sure to do at least a small maintenance exercise so I can check my imaginary box. You can always make it a real box if you like to-do lists. Or you can drop a Czechoslovakian immigrant into a cardboard box if you're in a Zucker Brothers movie.

MAKE REGULAR DEPOSITS

Technically, this concept is applicable to any endeavor in which you have long-term commitments. I learned it from Trainer Tom as it applies to fitness, so I put it in this section because I am the king of this book. Quite simply, it's a metaphor for consistency. There are many times I absolutely do NOT feel like going in to exercise. Apartment Dojo is forty minutes from my house. I've been driving there for six years. Some days, I wake up and every cell in my body does its best to add weight to my organs to keep me pinned in bed. I go anyway. I have never canceled on Tom because I didn't feel like going. I know that if I ignore my brain and get my body to put on workout clothes and get in the car, I'll be fine once I'm there and getting blood to flow through my veins. And I always am, and I really DO leave feeling better.

As I have said, I struggled with a back injury since I was eighteen, so there were times when all we did was stretch. "It doesn't matter," Tom would say, "you showed up." A few workouts would go by and then I would have a stellar one. The kind where I didn't feel wrecked, I had tons of energy, and I experienced breakthrough moments. Tom would always point out that it was the sum total of all of the workouts that had gotten me to that moment. The crappy ones, he reasoned, were ESSENTIAL for getting to the good ones. He would also say that pushing through the tough workouts was when you learned the most about yourself. "Name one workout from last year!" he said to me once. "I . . . don't . . . schwaaa??" "EXACTLY!" (Tom gets charmingly excited while making a good point.) "It's not any one thing that changed your life. It's CONSISTENCY. You got to this place by showing up regularly, no matter how you felt!" If you can develop the ability to get through stuff that you don't feel like doing and come out of it stronger, how could that NOT bleed over into the rest of your life? How could you not become a force of Nature?

Think of your body as a bank account and today you open that account with zero dollars. Every time you do something positive for yourself from this day forward, whether it be exercising or eating healthier, you are making a deposit. Over time, those deposits begin to accumulate into quite a pile of goodness. The reason this is important is because there will ABSOLUTELY be times that you aren't able to do those things. You get sick, there's a work deadline, you're traveling, it's the holidays, whatever. The regular deposits that you make when you *can* give you a cushion for those times when life sucks you down into its undertow. As I complainbrag often, I travel a lot. Traveling DARES you to eat well. Like, double-dog dares you. It is VERY tricky to not eat like shit when you're grabbing quick food on the road or in airports. And the Midwest and the South—while I love them—by and large have not embraced the whole "Don't eat the worst stuff you can imagine" thing yet. I ordered an Asian chicken salad from the "lite menu" in Kansas once and got a salad with fried chicken, wonton strips, and globs of ranch dressing—you know, the way the Asians eat it. Caucs will put ranch dressing on anything and everything: meat, vegetables, other ranch dressing. They don't care. Ranch dressing contains the molecule that gives white people their pasty, reflective sheen.

Because I know there will be many moments in my life when I can't eat the way I'd like to, I do my best to stay on top of it when my life is a little more regulated at home. This way, I don't have to feel bad for falling off the wagon when life happens. The same is true for exercise. If you exercise two or three days a week—week in, week out—you will be totally fine if you go through a few weeks or a month when you can't. Tom reminds me CONSTANTLY: You can't get into shape in a week, you can't fall out of shape in a week. When you have a spell where workouts are impossible, you're never more than two or three workouts away from getting back to where you were. This is GOLDEN information for someone like me, who tends to catastrophize. "Aw SHIT! I haven't worked out in three weeks! It's over! I'm gonna get all doughy and huffy again!" This is untrue. It's important to know this because when you haven't worked out for a few weeks your brain will try to talk you out of going back. If you feel like "it's all over," you're less likely to start doing it again. This, as it turns out, is an empty excuse.

Making deposits is all about building credit. When you make the choice to be extra nice to people every day, they are much more forgiving that one day when venom shoots out of you because you were on an all-night flight next to an unhappy baby. (Babies—or "crypods" as I call them—would be SO AWESOME if you could set them on "vibrate.") This also applies to delivering quality work to the best of your ability on time. Employers will be lenient if you have a misstep here or there, because we are imperfect beings. Make the deposits. Build your credit. If you can just do that for the rest of your life, you will have had a wonderful stint here on Earth.

Effort, big or small, is always rewarded! Deem yourself worthy and embrace that, which you so deserve.
—Trainer Tom

Now that you are on your way to a more physically capable you, give yourself another 50 XP for completing this section!

PART THREE

TIME

THINGS THAT ARE
BIGGER THAN YOU

Humans are a religious bunch. We love aligning ourselves with notions and simulacra because we need a path. Any path. We need an ideology to ferry us through life because decision making is a bit easier once we have a prefab belief system in place. This religion is usually, but doesn't have to be, Christ-y in nature. You can folmulate (a word I just made up: folmulate= follow + emulate) *Star Trek*, the Jedi, the Flying Spaghetti Monster, math, *WoW*, Monty Python, Unix philosophy, '80s teen comedies, cactus worship, NERDISM (see what I did there?) . . . it doesn't matter. It just has to be a system. Mine is primarily self-improvement. It's probably because I was such a fuckup in my twenties that I realized I needed to change my life in my thirties so my forties through deathies wouldn't suck.

This was an easy path to follow because there is no shortage of self-help literature. As a resident of Los Angeles, I spend much of my day ensnared in traffic. Our public transportation system is what experts would call "not awesome," so I spend a lot of time in my car. Many years of basic cable "celebrity" have afforded me a nice one, so I enjoy being wrapped up in it like a snazzy metal blanket. The main problem is that I am constantly bored of the music I already know I like. My thirst for new music is greater than the available new music that I can drink with my brain.

Then, in 2005, I had a stunning epiphany, which is almost shameful in its simplicity: Instead of mindlessly listening to music in my mobile exoskeleton, I can download self-improvement audiobooks so I can LEARN while I TRAFFIC. All of this commute time was fertile education soil just waiting to be seeded.

I began downloading—it didn't matter what—as long as it promised improvement in some way. I knew a lot of it might be sucky and ridiculous, but as long as I was committed to the idea of learning to improve, it was better than trying to harmonize with the same fifteen songs over and over (yeah, I try to harmonize with songs a lot, a practice that I'm sure you can assume is HIGHLY annoying to witness). I started noticing changes. Work was increasing in frequency and I was feeling happier about stuff in general. I had even stopped name-calling strangers in traffic ("shit-stick" being an old fave) because I knew that driving = learning. And learn I did! I began to create a patchwork of principles that suited me from each of the works. This was also the Bruce Lee method: Take what works from many different disciplines and chuck the rest ("chuck" as in "discard," not as in "Norris"—who, BTW, could discard YOU with nothing but a stare through a sandstorm if he so desired).

Because of this obsession I wrote a feature article for the January 2008 issue of *Wired* titled "Diary of a Self-Help Dropout," in which I followed three different productivity books for two weeks at a time each. They were David Allen's mega-bible *Get-*

ting Things Done, Julie Morgenstern's *Never Check E-Mail in the Morning* (I never got good at this), and Timothy Ferriss's *4-Hour Workweek*. Up to this point, most of my self-improvement studies had centered around goal setting and happiness. As I was getting busier than I had ever been, I knew time management was imminent, so I took on the project to study as much as to write snarky quips in a shiny magazine for money.

It was a success! My time-management skills improved dramatically. While I learned a few tips from the books I read, my biggest lesson came in turning inward and seeing where my time went, how I worked, what hours I was most productive, and what could help me stay organized. This journey really got me to examine and understand my own processes better. I not only discovered my own work rhythms but also figured out that managing time didn't just mean color-coding my calendar and identifying "time hijackers." I reasoned that any constructive thing I was able to accomplish was effectively utilizing my time in the best way possible; this encompassed things like goal setting, finances, and emotional organization. It's not just about compartmentalizing your clock but also making sure that you expend your time on things of value. Part of the reason my life was such a *Lusitania* was because I wasn't employing it to do things like "pay bills on time" or "maintain a sane living space." After your mind is calm and your body is fit, all that's left is to fill your time with worthwhile events that will pay off for you in your present and future.

FUN STORY TIME!

I became pals with Tim Ferriss after our interview for the *Wired* article. Tim's a solid human. Really nice, straightforward, and also a lover of comedy (we've had many a chat about Louie CK and Patton Oswalt). Early in 2009, I had gone up to San Francisco to perform in SF Sketchfest, an all-encompassing three-week-long comedy festival that showcases the best comedians, writers, and filmmakers, in this comedy Nerd's opinion. I called Tim a few weeks ahead of time and scheduled a lunch. Then the night of the scheduled lunch had arrived, and I realized I had forgotten to go to it. I had missed a lunch with one of the foremost time-management experts. Me = ANUS WHISTLE. What followed was the most sheepish, apologetic, and self-flagellatory (may not be a word) message. "I don't know what happened . . . I forgot to check my calendar because it's a weekend . . . PLEASE let me take you to lunch to make up for it." It was that awful sinking feeling of "I just fucked up by accident and there's nothing I can do about it."

A half hour later I got a call from Tim. "No problem at all," he said. "I had a lot of work to do anyway. Let's do it tomorrow." Yes! What a superior human! He totally let me off the hook. We went to lunch and had a great chat at a great restaurant. As we were leaving to finish our man-date, Tim stopped and said, "OK, I have to fess up about something . . . I forgot about yesterday, too." That hung in the air for a minute. Then the laughing and ball-busting kicked in. "Well done, Ace!" "Promise you won't tell anyone," Tim chuckled. (He has since released me from my vow.) The point is, I was hell-bent on managing my schedule. Tim is a time-management consultant, among other things. We both spaced this event. You will space things. No matter how in control you think you are, there will be times when you miss the mark. Everyone fucks up sometimes. Go easy on yourself as you start to organize your time. #RecurringTheme

SET UP YOUR OWN POST OFFICE: PRESORT YOUR MAIL

Well, since most modern communication revolves around electronic mail, let's start there! So how do you manage the avalanche of sadness that is your daily in-box? With a system, of course! If every morning a machine dumped all of your food on your face at once, do you think you would ever eat breakfast? Chances are you'd question the invention of that cursed machine and why you traded money for it in the first place. This machine is your computer. Without a good email sorting system in place, it is essentially dumping on your face.

Do you have one in-box that all of your mail piles into? WHY WOULD YOU DO THIS TO YOURSELF? In this delivery system, every time you open your email it's like that cliché where someone opens a messy closet and it buries them in junk. Unless you can set up a mini digital post office that keeps your in-box manageable, you're always going to feel like all of your email is in one giant litter box.

FIRST, do you have a Gmail account? You should. It has the best spam filters, in this Nerd's opinion. Also it's free, configurable, and you get a ton of storage. (More if you pay a small annual fee!) I run all of my accounts through it, even the Nerdist .com ones. If you set it up to come through a mail client like Microsoft Outlook, Mozilla Thunderbird, or Apple's native mail program then it will be more backed up than if you just use the web portal, which is not at all. If you have a work email that sits on your back in an oppressive manner, get a separate personal email. This will keep your business emails out of your personal life and vicey versey. Next, set up another Gmail account for non-interpersonal correspondence. Invest $0 in one and start giving it out to any Web site, bank, or utility company that wants to send you information about your account or "special offers." Then go back to your main Gmail. Click the little gear icon and select "Mail Settings." Under the "Accounts and Import" tab, tell Gmail to pull in your extra accounts mail. I could explain it here, but it is VERY easy and self-explanatory when you get there. Once you've done this, click the "Labels" tab. Scroll down past "System Labels" to "Labels." Create a label for correspondence from companies that will try to continually sell you stuff because you bought something from them once. I call mine "Lists," because they're usually lists I didn't ask to be on. Use whatever word makes you happy. Now scroll all the way to the bottom and look for the tiny hyperlinked phrase "Create a new filter." Here you'll see a bunch of fields that represent the different fields of an email: From, To, Subject, and so on. The idea here is to set up an email rule that directs any email coming from the red herring email address into the "Lists" folder. In the "To" field, enter your red herring email and click "Next Step." On the vertical list, select the checkbox next to "Skip the Inbox (Archive It)," then select the one next to "Apply the Label" and select your "Lists" label. On the bottom right, check "Also Apply Filter to XX Conversations Below" and click "Create Filter." And there you have it! Now, some of the more hard-core Nerds reading this book will "Pffffft, no shit" at this, but I am surprised how many people I know that I think are pretty Nerdy but don't think to sort their mail with email rules. Remember, most of the companies that you give your email to will sell it to annoying greedy spammers so this move alone will cut your in-box junk down by a million percent (could be a half million percent—again, individual results may vary).

This one is a little more obscure, and doesn't always work with companies who ask for your email address, but it's worth a shot. Gmail allows you to add + identifiers to your email address when you give it out. In other words, if your email is wienerpants@gmail .com, you can tag it thusly: wienerpants+bank@gmail.com. Emails to this address will still come to your main inbox, but the + identifier allows you to sort mail with that tag more efficiently. Following the steps above, just tell Gmail that whenever that specific +tag comes through it should sort it into a label of your choosing. Again, some companies' email entry systems are confused by +tag and will scold you to enter a valid email address (but I AM, you robotic asscan!). If the tag doesn't work, instead add a "." anywhere in your Gmail address. Ever get someone else's email that has your name but it looked different? If you have VernSpermly@gmail.com, you will also get mail addressed to Vern.Spermly@gmail.com. Or V.ernSpermly@gmail.com. Or V.e.r.n.S.p.e.r.m.l.y@gmail.com. If you don't wish to set up a separate account and go through that business, you can give out a dotted version of your Gmail address to jerks who want to sell you shit and create a filter with that specific configuration of your addy.

I first discovered the +tag years ago on Lifehacker (lifehacker .com) and I cannot recommend that site enough. There is a wealth of articles on how to streamline your digital life, and the people who blog and run it are a nice bunch of Nerds who will give you all sorts of tech tips. The first time you go there, say good-bye to your day because you will get sucked into one great article after another.

ARCHIVE!

Gmail's archive feature is your digital closet. Every few weeks, I make sure that my in-box is full of stuff that I've taken care of, or I star the things that still need attention and move topic-specific emails into corresponding labels. Then I select the empty checkbox that floats above the vertical row of checkboxes. A notice will pop up: "All 50 conversations on this page are selected. Select all XX conversations in Inbox" (the latter phrase will be hyperlinked). I select it and consequently it selects every piece of mail in my inbox. Then I click the bolded "Archive" button in the menu bar just above my emails. They are sent to a label called "All Mail," which is accessible and searchable whenever, and my in-box is CLEAN. An empty inbox won't last long if you're a busy person, but it sure feels niiiiiiiiiice.

SNAIL MAIL

Though its title is somewhat speciest (species racist) toward the shelled molluscan gastropods, piles of mail manage to find their way into every crevice like so much shit glitter. It STILL happens in my life. Not a week goes by and somehow a fresh drift of unopened bills and solicitations blanket my workspace. The obvious solution is to open your mail and deal with it the second you get it. This, of course, is not always a possibility. Here's what I try to do:

Eliminate Mail at the Source!
- Opt out of every credit card company list.
- Set bills on "autopay" and/or select "paperless billing."

Gather 'n' Sort!
- If you have time to grab your mail, you have time to quickly drop it into three piles: junk, not junk, and unknown.
- Push the junk pile into your shredder.
- Open the unknowns first, because they are most likely shrouded junk and can be tossed.

Set It and (Don't) Forget It!
- Quickly prepare anything that requires action for the next step.
- If it's a bill, remove the extraneous leaflets, tear off at the perforation, and shred it. (PS—you should have a shredder to protect your identity from sentient garbage rats.)
- Pair the piece you need with its accompanying envelope.
- Place all of your "waiting for next step" mail in a neat pile near your checkbook (I put mine between my keyboard and monitor) so that when you have time, all you have to do is write a check or respond to that wedding invitation with a "YES" and "CHICKEN."

TRACKING YOUR TIME

So we've established that time slips through your dainty fingers like a slick water weenie, so how can you begin to get a handle on it for output purposes? The title of this chapter might offer you a little clue. Or the actual answer. YOU MUST TRACK YOUR TIME. Before you start trying to schedule productivity, it is vitally important that you see where your time is going on an average day. Any good scientist knows (you will become a scientist of time) that you can't start experimenting until you have some data as your Point A. It is SO much easier to change that which has been quantified. Download the free timer at NerdistWay.com (or whatever clock you have the strongest bond with) and over the course of a day click it every time you start doing something different. The clock comes with a ruled text field, so type in whatever that new thing is each time. THIS INCLUDES EVERYTHING. "Answered emails," "Went on Etsy to find clown paintings," "Played Angry Birds while pooping," whatever you do. I want you to see *exactly* where your time goes each day so you then can start manipulating it. Sculptures are not very compelling without clay. (Except for ice sculptures. They're beYOOtiful.) This time chart will be your clay and your schedule is the sculpture you'll end up with.

When you see your whole day broken down and measured, you will begin to see gaping holes where you could be focusing on important things like furthering your career and contributing to society. And, of course, figuring out where to put your dick-around time. When you can learn to do this, your schedule will become modular units of time that you can place in any order you see fit. The clouds will part, animals will sing, and you'll surf a beam of light up into the sky to high-five your deity of choice.

CHARACTERCIZE

 Track your time in a day.

 Write down how long you spend on each activity.

 Marvel at the results!

MODULAR SCHEDULING: 1, 2, 3!

"Look, you douche with strategically messed-up hair, I REALLY don't have any free time!!!" you say.

Even if you already categorize yourself "a busy human," I guarantee you will still find capsules of free time that you didn't notice were there. Here's how: If you did the previous Charac-tercize, you'll find that a percentage of it is devoted to drifting off, spacing out, or even worse, false productivity. "False productivity" is a silent killer, and the web is MASTERFUL at it. You see, gentle reader, the web tricks us into thinking we're accomplishing something because we are constantly absorbing information. To our brain, we are indeed learning stuff, it's just usually not stuff we can apply to our professional lives or betterment. Here's a typical example, ripped from the pages of my own life (from "Diary of a Self-Help Dropout," *Wired*, issue 17.01, Jan '09):

My girlfriend informs me that there's a black widow nesting in a drainpipe near our garage. I have now been on the *GTD* program for several days and am a next-action machine. I say out loud to myself in a robot voice, "Processing . . . dot dot dot . . ." I head outside, already planning my next action: "Pour water down drain to send spider on river rampage to Jesus." On the way, however, I discover a dead squirrel. Protocol interrupted. How do you dispose of a dead squirrel? I return to the house with my bucket of water to ask the Internet. A state of California Web site informs me that I have to call the West Nile Virus Hotline. WTF?! I open a new tab and Google "West Nile deaths human California." Only one this year. Next action: Let air out of lungs. Back to westnile.ca.gov. From the photos, I identify the decedent as a Fox squirrel. While scrolling through, I notice that its cousin the Douglas squirrel is adorable! I throw it—the words, not the squirrel— at Wikipedia. *Pine squirrel located in the Pacific coastal states.* Huh. I jot down "pine squirrel" for use in as-yet-unwritten funny sentence. Back to the 'pedia. Naturalist John Muir described the Douglas squirrel as "by far the most interesting and influential of the California sciuridae." . . . Sciuridae?

How has that term managed to elude me for more than three decades? I click the link and learn that it's a family of large rodents—squirrels, chipmunks, marmots, and, uh, spermophiles. I wonder how you pronounce it. sky-yer-EE-dye? SURE-i-day? Goto: Merriam-Webster Online. Damn—it's a premium-account word. I'll have to slum it on Dictionary .com. Aha! sigh-YURi-day. I say it aloud several times, nodding with a false sense of accomplishment. The black widow is still alive. The Fox squirrel is still dead. And so are 35 minutes of my life.

The Web is exactly that—a sticky web of unproductivity that can paralyze you the farther into it you go.

Once you have tracked all of your time for a day, give each item a rating of 1, 2, or 3. 1 = THING THAT NEEDS TO BE DONE IMMEDIATELY, 2 = THING THAT NEEDS TO BE DONE BUT NOT URGENTLY, 3 = DICK-AROUND TIME (I guess I lied about not using it again). This rating system can sometimes be challenging for Nerds because part of their DNA is placing HEAVY importance on things that seem essential but really are not. We tend toward OCD, without being quite unfortunate enough to have it. It's like we're in a rickety sloop perpetually circling OCD Island, but we never actually dock there. (Though if you're counting to ten over and over as you circle you may have it.) The point here is, do your best to have an objective eye on your actions.

This kind of numerical prioritizing was greatly helpful to me after I was able to figure out my productivity threshold. Mine is roughly an hour, which means I'm good to spew out hot jets of viscous information for about sixty minutes before my brain gets flaccid. Were I to graph it, it would be a sine wave. When I sit down to work (like the writing of these very words, say), it always starts off a little slowly as the gears and cranks begin to turn and drive each other, but after a few minutes I hit that zone where the world melts away and my typing fingers are merely a conduit from my thoughts to the digital page. At about the forty-five-minute mark, I start to lose focus. I start to drift off a tad, maybe noticing things on my desk or emails that came in. Then I have to go back and reread what I just wrote because I forgot it already. At this point, I know it's time to take a break. I'm fine with that because I expect it. Now I can either do number 3 (back to searching for squirrels) or tackle a number 2 (either the priority rating or the dirtier way you could read that). And if I can't seem to get in a zone or I get out of one, I can always change environments.

TIMECOP: BE YOUR OWN POLICE FORCE

I'm not trying to rob you of your dick-around time. You need dick-around time. If you don't decompress in some way your brain will explode against the walls of your skull and the only time-management schedule you'll be on is right after coloring time, when you take the pink pill that tastes like happy. The mission here is to better plot out your day so that you allow yourself some guilt-free dicking around. If you're a freelancer or work independently within a company or organization, you are in charge of ALL OF THIS. If you work in a standard nine-to-five-type job, your slightly different task will be compartmentalizing your corporate projects to allow yourself room for outside passion projects or other things that require structured time.

There's no complicated scheme. It boils down to this: *Policing yourself is easy when you have a goal.* The actual police use "the law" as their goal. Or even "drunkenness on power." Figuring out your goals is easier than it sounds, and you certainly wouldn't have purchased this book if you weren't a white-hot pack of fire-crackers with a can-do attitude. Once again, invoke the Dark Lord Charlie Rose! That's it. Just take your brain aside and ask it some of those really good questions!

Your brain will spit out answers because it is a processing machine and that's what it's designed to do. You might even amaze yourself at the knowledge and ideas locked up in your cerebral Azkaban, just waiting to be sprung with a question or twelve. ALWAYS start with "What do I want?" You might get general answers like, "a billion dollars," "truckloads of sex," "a hover board," "unified field theory," and so on.

> SPECIFY!: One of the reasons you give up on goals is because the answer you get is too general and therefore too vast for your brain to process so it gives up. But don't let it. Break the goal down and ask more and more specific questions. Go back to Chapter 1 if you need help determining a goal. If you don't know an answer, pretend you are someone who does. I am a huge supporter of tricking yourself.

Once you have your goal in mind, use it as the framework of your law. Whenever you start doing something, check in with yourself to make sure that what you are about to do will take you in the direction of whatever goal you set. You'll know on a very deep level if the answer is yes or "But . . . lobster porn!"

CHARACTERCIZE

⚠ What tangible thing do I really want?

⚠ What emotional thing do I really want?

⚠ What resources do I currently have that will help push me in that direction?

⚠ What resources would I need to bring these to fruition?

⚠ Do I actually already have what I want and don't realize it? (This sometimes is true.)

KEEP A CALENDAR

I honestly don't know how the hell I ever got anything done before I started keeping a calendar. I think maybe I didn't exist before, like Buffy Summers's whiny kid sister, Dawn. If you want to have even a prayer of streamlining your time management, you have to give your life a structure. Even if you feel like you have nothing worth scheduling, you will subconsciously seek out ways to fill your calendar. Currently, I use iCal and MobileMe to sync it. (Chill, PC Nerds. You can like your own thing, too.) Google Calendar is also pretty terrific, and if you're running Android it will integrate the best. This is not going to be a long section because there's no need to overcomplicate this simple process.

Set up a personal calendar and a work calendar (my "Personal" is blue, "Work" is green). I wouldn't set up too many because most things will fall into one of those two categories. If you have more specifically recurring activities, then go ahead and add them as calendars (I have separate "Travel" and "Stand-up" calendars), but be careful not to overcategorize. You don't want it to be messy with colors.

My friend Alex, in addition to having a great calendar setup, also has a corkboard with all of his current projects pinned on three-by-five note cards. This gives him a bird's-eye view of pretty much everything that will absorb his attention in the present. (Corkulous is a great iPad app that will make a digital version of this for you.) It's great because when he finishes working on a project, he never has to think, "Okayyyyy . . . what now?" He knows exactly what to pop over to next. Plus, it has the added bonus of showing you that you ARE involved in real projects. This is excellent for your self-esteem and motivation.

Once you get everything up, set up automatic sync for all of your devices. This has become probably the most important feature for the modern individual. To swiftly dart through your busy life, you need your data to be consistent. Rather than waste pages going through stuff you can easily find on the webs, just search "calendar sync" on your device and software. Chances are, you're running iOS or Android, so MobileMe (more 'spensive but better for Apple devices) and Gcal (free and better for Android). If you run Outlook, Google also offers Google Calendar Sync to get you sorted out. You're a Nerd, so you probably know all of this and probably have a decent system already with your specific device or platform configuration. Probably.

GOOD BUSY, BAD BUSY, AND FUN TIMES

I enjoy busy. I have not been busy at times in my life, and I did not enjoy those times. I think we're designed to strive for busy because being busy usually signals progress. The problem is,

Nerd minds typically don't distinguish between "good" busy and "bad" busy, but if you want to be all productive and shit, you should. When trying to determine which value an activity falls under, use this handy guide. Cut it out of your book and tape it to your monitor if you have to:

Good Busy: Anything that moves you closer to your goals.

Bad Busy: Anything that does not involve your goals or move you closer to them in any way, pushing you instead into a cul-de-sac of unproductiveness. Tim Ferriss calls this "procrasturbating," a word I'm jealous I didn't come up with.

Now, BAD BUSY can also equal "fun times" → playing video games, mindlessly surfing the webs, looking for animal faces in ceiling tiles, whatever you do to check out. Fun times are important because you need to decompress, but when fun times start eclipsing "good busy," that's when they become "bad times." Now listen to "Best of Times" by Styx.

So how do you keep the voracious FUN TIMES from devouring your productivity? Simple, Nerd! You schedule it! Now, I'm sure that your child glands will initially reject this idea because it might seem that scheduling fun is some kind of square thing that account executives do in between spreadsheets. WHILE THAT MAY BE TRUE, that doesn't make it any less of an excellent thing to do. In your calendar program, add a calendar devoted only to fun activities. Make it orange or something if you want it to feel "wacky" because you're "a real card."

The advantage to scheduling your fun time is that you NEVER have to feel guilty about it. You've EARNED it. Also you'll appreciate it more and it will motivate you to work harder to get to it.

CHARACTERCIZE

 Tag your common activities as "Good Busy" or "Bad Busy."

 Make sure you have a proper balance that you are sure is moving you in the direction you want to go.

RELAXING

Truthfully, I am TERRIBLE at this. In full disclosure, I try to do it, but my mind always drifts back to work. In a perfect scenario, I would take regular vacations. When I have indeed done this, it was because I put it in the calendar and STUCK TO IT. There's always going to be something, a reason not to go. But you HAVE to do it. Recharging is an important part of brain maintenance. If you're busy all the time, it's important for your self-image to reward yourself. I'm sure you have an authority figure in your life from whom you cherish praise and emotional rewards, but I think the most important person to look to for rewards is yourself. It's about acknowledging that you're on the right path and that you approve of your actions. It will reinforce your decision making and clear your head for new ideas.

Whatever your work environment may be, try to make your vacation environment the OPPOSITE. Mix it up. If you work in a big city, take a nature trip. If you're in the verdant Pacific Northwest, go to a beach or take in the Great Plains. (BTW, as a touring comic I have to recommend being a tourist in America. I have seen so many wonderful places in this country that most people wouldn't think of when choosing a vacation. We are a diverse land and people. Just don't order that Asian chicken salad in Kansas.)

CHARACTERIZE

 Write down some ways you can relax.

 Plan your dream vacation in detail.

 Use it as a goal to motivate you.

HOW TO CONTROL TIME

You can't control time in a *Doctor Who* fashion, jumping forward and back, across dimensions, doing really cool things with a flying police box (damn, I WISH!!!). But you can control the SPEED of time. Not absolute time, but relative time. I believe the latter matters as much as, if not more than, the former.

How many of your friends have said to you recently, "Man! This year has just FLOWN by! What the hell happened??" The last few years seem to have moved at an unbelievable pace, to the point where it feels difficult to grasp sometimes. So what DID happen? Did the space-time continuum start going to universe raves and doing meth? That would be rad. The more likely answer is that technology happened. The dawn of the smartphone era happened. Once Apple changed the game and everyone else followed suit, we became a culture of beings with fully functioning web-enabled devices. At any given moment, we have access to the sum total of human knowledge. Granted, we don't often use the Internet to tap this knowledge. Though I do occasionally Google things like "What did Julius Caesar eat for breakfast?" while waiting in a long line, I'm more apt to check Facebook requests, check Twitter, or tweet something snarky about how long the line is.

It's web access and social networking. If a watched kettle

continued

never boils then I promise it only takes a second while you're checking Stephen Fry's status updates (which are unendingly delightful, BTW). The constant distraction of being connected is robbing us of our time. More specifically, it's robbing our AWARENESS of time. Ultimately, if an hour feels like ten minutes, isn't that important? What good is an hour if you lack the awareness to experience it? I can recount numerous times in 2010 when I was playing Fieldrunners and realized "Well, whaddaya know? I've been doing this for three hours."

Concentrated game blocks aren't the enemy, but filling every available minute connected to a computing device in some way can be. Notice how, when you start downloading a file, you get an "estimated time remaining"? How often is it accurate to absolute time? Almost never. It may jump from "an hour remaining" to "4 minutes remaining" and everywhere in between. This is due to a variety of factors, naturally, like connection speed, traffic on the server in your area, and traffic on the server from which you're downloading the file. The point is that web time is intrinsically distorted, and it has interesting parallels with how we perceive time while connected to it.

I'm not recommending a total freeze. If you want time to go faster, by all means distract yourself at all times. Your life will soar by. Just know, though, that if you feel compelled to always be distracted you might be avoiding something emotionally, and you might want to have a chat or several with a therapist. It's humanly counterintuitive to wish your life to expire faster. On the contrary, if you want to feel time crawl, go live in a cabin for a month with no technology. Or get arrested and go to jail. Ya see, prison could actually FREE you from your self-constructed TIME PRISON in a flippity-floppity *twist* at the end and blah blah blah M. Night Shyamalan.

While pursuing your goal of time-lordery, you shouldn't have to take one or the other extreme, but as long as you know that you can extend the sensation of time by unplugging at regular intervals and simply becoming more AWARE of it, you shouldn't feel as cheated of your minutes and hours when popular social markers like "New Year's Eve" or "my fucking birthday" come around. Be mindful to inject some nuggets of quality into your time to enhance its value.

CHARACTERCIZE

 Spend one day with no Internet and see if you feel a difference in the length of the day.

BECOME AN EVIL GENIUS

Yes! YOU! The time has come for you to take your place as a plotter of plots and a doer of deeds, all under the auspices of a grand master plan. Evil geniuses get an exceptionally bad rap, but any reasonable person would have to admit that they drive a good story forward because they are momentum in human (usually) form. Granted, some can be a pain in the ass—what with their carelessly snuffing out innocent lives in the selfish pursuit of their desires and all—but when you dissect their mental DNA, you find an EXCELLENT time manager that is willing to stop at nothing to achieve greatness.

Evil geniusing has a long and storied history dating back millions of years to Davor Tosselrack, an australopith who threatened to break the sun with a rock were the sum of one million unmarked tubers not paid to an off-continental account. He was later devoured by hyenas in a bar fight. I may have made a lot of that up, but one thing is for sure: Nerds make great evil genii. An evil genius is nothing more than a Nerd with a tragic revenge story.

NERD + TRAGEDY = EVIL GENIUS

While I can't recommend wiping out California for beachfront Arizona property and killing millions in the process, I can recommend taking an evil genius approach to your life and career. ATTN CRAZY PEOPLE: DO NOT use this as an excuse to hurt people. This is a metaphor intended to give you motivation and focus. This is "fun evil" not "evil evil."

Superheroes are jocks. Most of them are pretty and have powers. (Except for Batman, but I think he was an evil genius who happened to perform a service congruent with our social standards. Really, he's a sociopath—a Dexter before there was a Dexter.) Evil geniuses work their way up. They are not afraid to plan big and take chances that most of the populace would deem "maniacal." They also take setbacks as motivation and retooling opportunities. In their mind, failure is simply not an option. "I'll get you next time, Gadget! Next tiiiiiiiiime," blurts a fist-shaking Dr. Claw.

These geniuses are onto something.

Why? Here's why! Among other things, evil geniuses (genii?):

1. Are highly motivated. A pivotal moment early in life dealt them a terrible blow. Rather than just "getting over it" the evil genius stewed and plotted to fill the hole that was left in the wake of that event. It reverberates to their very core and haunts them daily. They are HIGHLY motivated to get the revenge they so desperately deserve.

2. Have a goal. Everything an evil genius does is part of a pathway to a singular vision. He doesn't just steal diamonds for the hell of it, with no follow-up plan. The diamonds are necessary to power the Sonic Disruptor, which will render inert the company that fired his father so many years ago, which ultimately led to his suicide and the orphaning of the evil genius (at the time, just a Nerdy kid).

3. Have a strong point of view. Years of torment and introspection have brought the Evil Genius closer to himself. He wishes to brand his indelible mark upon the world and be forever remembered. To do this, he has to be specific enough and have easily identifiable symbols that define him.

4. Never give up. Whether incarcerated or left for dead, the evil genius is in a constant state of "Until next time!!!" No matter how down the chips seem to be, he is never down until deceased and is forever plotting his next series of moves. He knows that his path of evil will encounter road blocks. He is not afraid to fail because ultimate success is the only option in his mind. This is accomplished by never giving up.

5. Undergo incredible transformations. Whether it be an unplanned chemical accident or just simple psychological trauma, evil geniuses usually start from a place of utter weakness and turn their lives around toward strength and the acquisition of power.

But how? HOW, I ASK YOU???

Well, think about it. If you're a Nerd, which you probably are, then you have felt weak in the past for one reason or another. Your archnemesis, in this case, should be the event or series of events that have seemingly conspired against you. You will mobilize your forces and begin plotting your revenge. No matter what you come up against, you will find a way around it because you are philosophically committed!

Another tactic is love. A number of evil geniuses are motivated by the unrequited love of someone. If they can only make a big enough splash . . . show him or her how truly spectacular they are, then he or she will be convinced!!! True, this rarely works in terms of getting the other person into the ol' sackeroo, but the trick here is to take advantage of the motivational feelings that this inspires. Freud said that we are motivated by two things: the desires for greatness and sex. Dale Carnegie recommended channeling sexual energy to motivate. It's an interesting idea, repurposing chemically induced emotions to achieve our Will. I like it. Gives the user a sense of control. It's also fun to trick your body. "Ha, Brain! You thought I was just trying to get laid! In fact, I was using your adrenaline surges to build an empire (to ultimately get laid)!" Try it. Fix someone in your mind you want to have sex with. Pick whoever you want, but I suggest that it be someone you're not likely to meet, like an actor or actress or a fictional wizard or witch. Make it a unicorn with six human tits for all I care. The point is, if it's someone you actually know, you might accidentally get obsessed with them and get all creepy. We don't want awkwardness and restraining orders in our master plan. Once you have that image, imagine yourself with that person. Imagine what it would be like, and what it would take for you to get that person's attention. (NO SHOOTINGS ALLOWED. I'm looking at YOU, Hinckley.) You'll most likely feel a tingly rush and a surprising amount of "get up and go!" A can-do attitude that is ready to spring into action to make this union happen. Now assume that whatever goal you have or task you need to complete will get you that much closer to making the relationship a reality. The other benefit of picking someone famousy is that, because it's a fantasy, it will free your mind from limiting yourself. People come up with fantastic ideas when in fantasy mode because in a fantasy anything is possible so you tend to get more creative. Some of those fantasies you'll find are actually attainable, but you never would have allowed yourself to think outside the box while living in reality. Here's a great nonsexual example: The fantastic geek merch site Think Geek.com would come up with fake products to "sell" on April Fool's Day. On April 1, 2009, the Nerd and Geek communities came together in their mutual holy-shittedness when they awoke to see the Tauntaun sleeping bag. The Tauntaun, I'm sure you know, is an omnivorous bipedal reptomammal indigenous to the ice planet Hoth, and in *Star Wars Episode V: The Empire Strikes Back*, Han Solo cuts one open and shoves Luke inside to keep him warm, effectively using it as a sleeping bag. Of course, it wasn't Think Geek's intention to sell them originally, just to trick Nerds, so they designed products with no limitations. They didn't have to worry about how the thing would get made, only that it would be a supercool Nerd fantasy product. Of course, the outcry was enormous and they ultimately found a way to make and sell them (smell not included).

A career founded on the evil genius platform can be as satisfying as it is lucrative. Intense, guided passion aimed at a nearly limitless goal is the idea. Once you pick a direction, unleash the fury that is you. They'll pay! OHHHH, how they'll all pay . . . You'll do things because your work will be valuable! And as I said before, success is THE BEST revenge with the least likelihood of jail time. Now that you are resolved (possibly) to begin crafting your nefarious (figuratively speaking) plans in your lair (literal), let us put those wheels in motion with the driveshaft of intention, THE CHECKLIST.

MASTERING YOUR DOMINION (A CHECKLIST)

- ☐ Pick a person or event that dominated you and made you feel small.

- ☐ Aim your rage and insecurities at that entity (but only in your mind, DO NOT hunt them down for reals).

☐ Come up with a goal: What ultimate thing do you want? Think big. You can always pare it down later. Write it down in your Character Tome. Cackle if necessary.

☐ Come up with a handful of ways you could achieve this goal. The more detail, the better. Wring hands together with accompanying cackles of increasing volume and length.

☐ Make a commitment to execute at least one action every day to move you toward this triumph.

☐ Transform your workstation into a lair or much smaller lairette.

☐ Post an image of said person or event in said lair or lairette.

☐ Whenever you feel lazy, or like you want to give up, look at that image and say or think, "No, fuck YOU" or "Curses! Ya ain't gonna bleed me, ya ruddy drip!" (if you prefer the drama of '30s gangsterisms to simple swears).

☐ Decide that you shall prevail no matter what. (This is most important.)

☐ Toast yourself in triumph. Monologue your plan to your pets if need be.

☐ Repeat as necessary.

TRACKING YOUR FINANCES

In my twenties—before I was responsible (presponsible?)—I had ruined my credit. Scorched-earth kind of stuff. Why am I bringing this up in Part 3 "Time Management"? Because I NEVER paid stuff on time, sometimes because I didn't have enough funds, other times because I just didn't give a shit. In Grown-Up World, this does not play out well. It turns out that your credit score has a lot of say over what you do, what jobs you can get, what you can rent, and what you can buy in this modern economy.

So there I was, thirty-one, newly sober and lookin' to make my life all sunny. The main problem was, my credit score was low. Equifax, TransUnion, and Experian are like three ravenous harpies fighting for a grip on your short hairs. Sucky or not, that's just the way it is [Hornsby piano hook], some things will never change [and other lyrics that are applicable that I don't remember]. Every time I applied for something they would actually pull out a boom box and play the "bom bom ba-bom, waaaaaaaahhh" brass section hit that people who lose on *The Price Is Right* get. (BTW, I always thought that show should be called *How Much Is This Shit?*) I had lapsed accounts and numerous really late accounts that were equivalent to a virtual poop smear all over the face of my purchasing power. I decided that I had to fix it. Clearly, it was tied to my identity and represented chubby-drunk Chris Hardwick, so naturally I needed to refresh it.

TIME TO FIX YOUR CREDIT

I'm not going to lie . . . if you have messed-up credit, it's a bit of a process to repair it. NOT IMPOSSIBLE, though, so don't get bummed. It just takes a little diligence and time. I wouldn't waste your money on credit repair bureaus. You'll just be paying them a bunch of money to do stuff you can do yourself.

First off, you have to make the decision to commit to perfect credit. It will act as a backbone when you start wondering whether or not you should put another video game on your already swollen Visa card.

Secondly, you're going to need to know how bad or not bad the situation is. Reality isn't mutable until you identify it! Get your credit report. At the time, I just paid some online service or other to get reports from all three companies at once. This probably wasn't the best approach. By law, the big three are REQUIRED to give you a free copy of your credit report every twelve months. Even if you have "good" credit, it's a smart idea anyway onaccounta rampant credit fraud and such.

Consumer credit is governed by the Federal Trade Commission, so for any legal credit questions you may have to just go to their Web site (ftc.gov) and type "credit" into the search bar. You'll get a list of pages that address such matters. According to their site, AnnualCreditReport.com is the only site sanctioned by the government, and not to be fooled by shifty or non-English imitators. If you've gotten your report within the last twelve months, the bureaus will also provide you with a free copy if you've recently been turned down for credit.

Once I had my reports, I went through them to assess the damage. There was a lot, so I noted all of the negatively reporting companies. Then I made a file for all of my reports and correspondence. (It's as thick as two Harry Potter books today.) My strategy was one of mild harassment. I wrote the following form letter:

> Dear [Company that has my balls in a vise]:
> After recently reviewing my credit file, I have noticed that you
> are reporting [ACCOUNT NUMBER] as a "Negative
> Account." As I have paid this account on [DATE: specific dates
> are always good] and have enclosed a copy of the document that
> supports this. Please adjust your reporting to my credit file
> accordingly.
>
> Most sincerely,
> Chris Hardwick

Then I sign it, because that seems official for some reason.

Note: If you have not paid the account or do not have proof, you can request that they verify the information they're reporting. Sometimes it's wrong.

Here's an example of a response I received several weeks later:

ROBINSONS · MAY

A DIVISION OF THE MAY DEPARTMENT STORES COMPANY

July 18, 2005

Mr. Christopher Hardwick

███████████████████
███████████████████

Re: 84-0447-0273

Dear Mr. Hardwick:

We are in receipt of your recent request to update the information being reported to your credit profile. We have reviewed your account records and wish to advise you that we have requested the credit bureaus to which we subscribe to change the rating on the above-referenced May Company account from "delinquent" to a "paid in full" status.

Please be advised that while it may take up to 60 days for the bureaus to complete this change, you may use this letter for verification, should you need to provide a potential credit grantor with proof that this correction is in process. After that time, you may wish to confirm that this correction has been made by directly contacting the credit bureaus. They are as follows:

Experian	Trans Union	Equifax
P. O. Box 2002	2 Baldwin Pl.	P. O. Box 105873
Allen, TX 75013-0036	P. O. Box 1000	Atlanta, GA 30348
(888) 397-3742	Chester, PA 19022	(800) 685-1111
	(800) 888-4213	

Thank you for the opportunity to be of assistance in this matter.

Sincerely,

Ebong Stancil
Account Services
May Credit Service Center
111 Boulder Industrial Dr.
Bridgeton, MO 63044

THE FOLLOWING STATEMENT MAY BE REQUIRED BY LAW: THIS IS AN ATTEMPT TO COLLECT A DEBT. ANY INFORMATION OBTAINED MAY BE USED FOR THAT PURPOSE.

I sent one every month or so to each company, apologizing and asking for clemency. Also a company isn't supposed to report you until you're thirty days late, but some of them cut this date close. If you have proof that you were NOT thirty days late, USE IT.

Next, I tracked down phone numbers. I called every so often and asked for the credit department. I asked for supervisors, anyone who would talk to me. I would plead my case. Granted, these people have heard it all, but at the end of the day they're humans, so the right one can help you. Some companies also will extend you a one-time courtesy of removing the first negative ding, so try that. This worked for me with Capital One. Be persistent. When in doubt with someone who won't budge, just randomly yell out, "FCRA!," or "Fair Credit Reporting Act!" It probably won't do much, but it'll make you feel like you're fighting for the little guy (or gal), which in this case is you. My belief is that even if all of this doesn't work, the effort you're putting in will help justify your resolve to follow through with the "living more responsibly" plan. The point is, now you're THINKING about this crap, where you probably never did before. That's grown-up-ed-ness.

After that, I contacted each of the credit bureaus and filed disputes. When you receive your credit report, you will get a phone number on it to deal with this very issue. Even though I was late on the payments, creditors still have to follow certain rules for reporting, so if they make even a tiny mistake, you have a case to get something removed. The other thing you can do is ask each bureau to add a statement to each negative reporting. This statement is your chance to plead your case to anyone who accesses your credit report. "I was hospitalized" or "This is being reported incorrectly, and I'm attempting to fix it," that sort of thing. It's preferable that it be true, so try to make that the case.

Most people don't know that they have the right to do this, so it makes you look a little sharper than everyone else.

Once you have done all of this, make sure to go through the whole process every year at the very least. At this point, it's a waiting game. I've heard that negative items can fall off anywhere between five and seven years. Truthfully, a creditor can knock it off whenever they friggin' feel like it, but most of them just won't. I begged some stony guy to the point of tears once to remove a ding on a closed credit card account. I was upset because I was so mad at myself for being so stupid for so many years, but I was absolutely committed to turning my life around. He coldly responded, "It is my experience that people don't change." It was shitty, but it strengthened my resolve, so thank you, asshole stranger, wherever you are.

Inquiries are another thing that people don't pay much attention to but should. Any time you apply for credit, it's recorded in the "Inquiries" section of your report. There's also a subsection that houses inquiries made by companies out looking for suckers, but don't worry about these. The only ones that matter happen when you are the one applying for credit. These will stay on your report for TWO YEARS, so try to keep this number limited. The more credit you apply for, the greater of a risk you appear to be. Why do you need so much credit suddenly? Are you trying to bilk some poor company out of their goods without paying? What are you buying over there? Is that a drug boat? Why are you drug boating??? These are rough and probably inaccurate examples of what a creditor might think while perusing your business.

The last bit of info you should straighten out on your report is your addresses. Creditors are likely to assume that having many addresses listed means that you're running from something. Now, you can't remove addresses that you've had that are correct, but a lot of times there are multiple variations of your addresses and sometimes at varying degrees of correctness. You don't need two versions that say "Apt 1" and "#1," so request that the credit bureau remove false or redundant versions of your addresses. This will help your score a tad, I'm told. Again, this stuff can be done via the contact info for each bureau on their respective credit reports. All of this stuff might feel overwhelming, but chip away little bits at a time. It took me three years, but it was a dang good victory when I finally got that clean report for the first time. It feels like being cured of finance herpes.

CHARACTERIZE
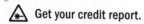

⚠ Get your credit report.

⚠ Write down the companies who are negatively reporting you.

⚠ Write down their correspondence info.

⚠ Communicate with them regularly.

⚠ Scratch them out as they get repaired.

GIVE YOURSELF SOME CREDIT (HAR HAR)

Some people will tell you to get rid of all your credit cards. This is not smart. Part of having a credit score is proving that you can use credit properly. Those who loan money want to know that you will actually carry at least a small balance (even if it's $30), because they make money charging you interest. I've been told (though exact algorithms for scoring are guarded secrets—pretty rad for the consumer, huh?) that small balances paid on time every month will improve your score. You don't want to carry a balance equal to or in excess of 50 percent of your allotted credit or you will be perceived as a risk. I held on to two credit cards with revolving credit (the pay-a-minimum-amount-every-month kind). I devoted a small percentage of my income to paying above the minimum payment each month to start getting those down.

Finally, I managed to get an American Express card. They're not paying me or anything. (But they SHOULD. At least one o' them shiny black cards that all the fancy people use! #1stWorld-Problems) My plan was that you CAN'T revolve credit on a green AmEx. You have to pay it off, in full, at the end of every billing cycle. This is ENORMOUSLY motivating to curb spending. With revolving credit, buying things just feels like you're throwing the payment into the stratosphere, and someday it'll fall back down, somewhere. It's ONLY a small amount, after all! By the time you get the bills, the momentum of several of these purchases will cut you into pieces, not unlike when pennies get tossed off a tall building and land on your skull. The other benefit to AmEx is that they have a decent reward system, though the "redeeming for travel" part of it doesn't always work out the way you'd want. (Airlines have VERY specific rules for the redemption of these points. It's doable, just pay attention to those rules.) In any case, your Nerdism will appreciate the point accrual aspect of it all.

BEFRIENDING TIME

After you've done all that you can do, you need to strap in and ride Time until your credit report is as clean as a Canadian pay toilet. (Those are actually very clean. I was very impressed in Toronto once. Hats off to you, Canada! Hey, stop leering at me

ON RESPONSIBLE USAGE OF TIME

An Open Letter from Doc Brown to Marty McFly

Dear Marty—

Having recently reviewed the surveillance footage of the events of the night you went back to 1985, I couldn't help but be slightly taken aback by your spurious reasoning of only allowing TEN FUCKING MINUTES to SAVE MY GODDAMN LIFE. Ten minutes??? Really. You actually thought that you could get from the Courthouse to Twin Pines Mall (I'm sorry, I mean LONE Pine Mall now—way to run over a tree, fucknut) in ten minutes. What the fuck did you think that could accomplish? What were you going to do? Vanquish the Libyans with your shortness? Yeah, I said it. YOU'RE TINY. Like the rat in Ratatouille (2008 reference), but in a puffy vest. Listen, you little feathered-haired leprechaun, any one of these Hill Valley MOUTHBREATHERS would have had the good sense to go back, oh, I don't know, AT LEAST A DAY to give me time to prepare for the Middle East extremists and their Summer of Love van of fucking DEATH, what with having a device that has mastered the dimension of TIME and all. And I'm INCLUDING Biff in that group. You are goddamn lucky that I have a compulsive disorder when it comes to taping paper back together. Otherwise you'd have been as useless as Einstein with a vernier caliper (smart joke—you wouldn't get it). Mark my words, Stuart Little, as SOON as I get this DeLorean up and running again (thanks for turning my car into a fucking lightning rod, BTW), I SWEAR I am going to go back and convince Jennifer to dump your Hobbit ass so you can go on that dumbshit camping trip ALONE with nothing to do but jam your little meerkat penis into that extra sleeping bag in the back of your gaywad new truck. Then I'm going to fuck her into tomorrow . . . LITERALLY. How long am I going to tap that skinny bitch? "Ten minutes oughta do it!" You vapid twat.

Thanks for watching me get shot twice,

Emmett "Doc" Brown

P.S.—You're a fucking CHICKEN.

like that, Montreal—or "Practice France" as I like to call you.) Waiting it out and living responsibly WILL start to pay off, and it is VERY satisfying. Of all the things in life that can't grant us 100 percent assurance, to know that your credit report HAS to right itself by law was incredibly comforting to me. When everything did finally fall off that finite conveyor belt, I may have gotten a little misty. Take care of your credit. Consumerism aside, it is a valuable lesson in patience, persistence, and responsibility.

TRACKING YOUR EXPENSES

It may not surprise you to learn that while I was busy ruining my credit, I was terrible with money. I always just had a vague sense that there might be some in there. I must have been spending at an alarming rate because one year in my twenties I made about $400,000 and it was all gone by the middle of the following year. #1stWorldProblemsAgain.

A few years later, when I starting cleaning stuff up, I decided that I needed to know where every cent was going. Only THEN could I adjust accordingly and NOT have "your debit card didn't go through" moments. I think most people would almost rather be punched in the neck than experience that. It's SO easily avoidable, as long as you do a little "ounce of prevention" work. (Nice one, Franklin! And I GET IT. You invented the post office. Stop looking so SMUG on the hundy, already.)

This thing I'm about to tell you may never have occurred to you to do, but when you see how frakking simple it is you might feel a light go on in your head. Or you'll think I'm a douche giving you obvious information. Either one of those. TRACK

YOUR FINANCES EVERY DAY. No, wait! Don't get mad! It's actually remarkably easy. You'll have a one-time emotional fee of setting everything up, but once you do, you'll auto-auto-AUTOMATE your way to a better YOU! In 2003, there wasn't much choice. I think there was Quicken, Microsoft Money, and spreadsheets. (I'm sure there were a few others but I can't remember.) I chose Quicken. I took statements as far back as I could find, which was 2002. Mind you, they were all unopened and in a box because I had not given much of a shit. I spent a weekend meticulously entering and categorizing. Business, Personal, Utilities, House, Auto, Tax—you don't need a ton of categories, and you can always make subcategories after you get flying. Also you don't really have to go back past the current tax year if you don't want to, but I recommend it. Once I had my marathon entering session (sounded sexier than I intended), I set up the automatic account update feature, which is as simple as a few menu navigations to link to your various accounts and credit card companies. Then I set it up to download new transactions every morning at 6:00 a.m. From then on, the first thing I would do every morning was go on to Quicken, see which transactions had downloaded, and make sure they were properly categorized. (Your regular transactions will properly categorize themselves.) This morning ritual took three minutes. And guess who NEVER AGAIN had to scramble at tax time to pull all of his shit together? → THIS GUY ←

Taking a few minutes of your time will save you piles of stress. You just export your info, email it to your accountant, send him any W2s you have, and you're DONE. With this method, you know how much you have and where every cent of it goes, at all times. You can even set savings goals and budgets. Again, once you have the numbers to look at, you can be the god of your finances. You will feel like the most responsible human you know!!!

<rant>Now, please don't think this is one big commercial for Quicken. It's not. In fact, they baffle me. When I switched over to Mac in 2007, the once robust finance tracking I had enjoyed on my PC was destroyed by Quicken for Mac 2007, a much less powerful program. It still worked, but it was a scaled down version of its PC brother because no one really took Macs seriously from 1985–1997 (their market share was still only in the single digits until the last few years). In 2010, I switched over to Quicken Essentials for Mac. It was a huge mistake and I don't recommend it. Puzzlingly, you cannot port a QE file to the PC version, so it is useless at tax time because guess who doesn't use Macs? ACCOUNTANTS. Maybe some do, but none that I've talked to. Even further, neither one of those are compatible with Mint (Mint.com), a wonderful online accounting program that Quicken's parent company Intuit purchased in 2009. All of this info is as of the writing of this book in early 2011, so maybe they'll start making decent decisions by the time it comes out. Personally, I'm running Parallels (a PC emulator) SOLELY to use Quicken for PC (which is SO good! That's why I don't understand the Mac slackage.). Because I run a business as well as the personal stuff, it's worth it. If you don't, and you have a Mac and aren't comfortable tracking your money in the cloud on Mint, then QE will do the job. Just export PDF reports to your accountant, if you have one. In theory it's good because the interface works with tags and looks like iTunes, but it just doesn't have that many features yet. Hopefully that will change.</rant>

Getting out of the Intuit family, I asked the Twitter Nerds who they were using and got this list. I have not used any of these, so I can't comment on their quality or effectiveness, but it'll give you some playtime screwing around until you find one that fits your needs:

GNUcash (gnucash.org): freeware, open source
FreshBooks (freshbooks.com): from $0–$39.95 per month; business and personal
QuickBooks (quickbooks.com): $229.95–$399.95; great for businesses
iBank 4 (iggsoftware.com/ibank): $59.99, also has investment tracking
Sage Peachtree (peachtree.com): $199.99–$A lot, depending on the size of the business
Twitter user @KraziRenee suggested "Rain Man"

There are a ton of other ones I had never heard of, and there's a fairly comprehensive list if you go to Wikipedia and search "accounting software." Just pick one. If you hate it, you can most likely export your data as a .csv file and import it into another program. Whatever you decide is probably better than what you're doing now.

HUGE SIDE NOTE: BACK UP YOUR ACCOUNTING FILE REGULARLY. If you only have one copy of the file and you lose it through a crash or for any reason, you will murder the creature in closest proximity.

SAVE SAVE SAVE

A book that changed my perception of money (and many people's perception of money) is called *The Richest Man in Babylon* by George S. Clason. You may have heard of it because most financial gurus have recommended it at one time or another. I'm not giving groundbreaking information here. It's an old book that is a quick, enlightening read, and it will give you some money goals and direction. It will teach you how to pay yourself first, with every bit of cash that comes your way. It will teach you the basics of planning and building and having a nest egg. Even if you feel like "I could NEVER do that," just try it and see anyway. I cannot properly encapsulate the feeling of watching your savings actually begin to grow if you're used to living paycheck to paycheck. This is the kind of shit that alters the direction of your life for the better. #HUGS

USE TRASHING TO SIMPLIFY YOUR LIFE

My life used to be a mess. I had accumulated a seemingly limitless assortment of toys, books, inoperative gadgets, and, of course, faded newspapers. The worst is gag gifts. Particularly when you're a comedian, people love to give you "hilarious" gifts: pens with boobs on them, Pol Pot bobbleheads, calendars with the Pope's head Photoshopped onto bikini models each month (I made up that last one). With gag gifts, you should be instantly allowed to throw it away in front of the giver. I mean, mission accomplished! We all had a laugh at the ridiculous nature of this novelty thing, so its value has been satisfied. Now I would like to rid myself of this otherwise useless toy before I am crushed under the weight of a pile of lolcat sweaters and penis-shaped drinking straws and some paramedics find me rotting there a few weeks later while muttering to each other, "Man, this guy sure loved cats and dicks."

For the longest time, I felt guilty about getting rid of any kind of gift. Surely it was a sharp slap to the cheek to dispose of something a friend had gone to the trouble of giving me (even though most gag gifts retail for under $25). With each move I managed to collect more and more boxes, like debris caught in a gravitational field of pointlessness . . . now all of this shite was starting to COST me money due to packing, move time, and storage. It was also costing me TIME. I was wasting gobs of it trying to find things or trying to reorganize my closets so that new piles of crap could Tetris into the old piles of crap. I felt strangely trapped . . . that is, until I discovered the organizational trick known as "trashing." Trashing is a process by which you take things that are in your house and place them somewhere else, where you have no responsibility for them anymore. The cornerstone of the trashing technique is local government–sponsored bins that are somehow emptied of their contents on a weekly basis. No one knows for sure exactly how it works, they just knows it works.

After years of personal research on hoarding, it turns out that old magazines serve no observable purpose; the information retrieval process on a stack of magazines is sucktarded *at best*, and uneven weight distribution makes them less than ideal for in-home fort building. I could give them to my neighbor, but he's a stuck-up jerk. You know who has no taste boundaries? **The Department of Sanitation.** They'll take anything I can cram in their cans (that sounds weird, but go with it).

So the next time you think about putting those extra unusable dock adapters that came with your new cell phone into a drawer simply because "you never know," you do know. You'll never use them. And the novelty bobblehead leader of the Khmer Rouge that someone gave you for your birthday is only fun the first second you see it. After that, it's another miniature roommate to deal with. Just because you have space doesn't mean you have to fill it. You don't jam old pennies and phone cords into your mouth and nose just because they'll fit there, do you? Well, do you??? ANSWER ME.

THE PAPER CHASE

The slow, malevolent revenge that trees have set upon us for slaughtering them and then writing on their skin has manifested through indoor forests of paper stacks now that decoupage our homes and offices, trying desperately to crush and suffocate us. Some of this elimination is easy because a lot of it is trash. But what about the stuff I NEED?? Insurance documents? Proof I paid my property taxes? Punny birthday cards from my mom?? I have tried for years to organize papers in a filing cabinet. I have tried various systems, from making folders that are subject based (Home, Bank, Office) to folders that are company based (AmEx, BofA, Farmer's Insurance), but the problem always lies in the fact that, at the end of the day, I'm just accumulating more paper. After five years, this shit gets annoying—bulging folders that tear at the hooks and fall in the drawer. I'd even clean them out every once in a while and put the oldest stuff in file boxes in storage, but then I'm just filling another space and having to pay money to do so. In my mind, there's no way around it. You just have to get rid of as much of it as possible using the two S's: SCAN and SHRED.

BYTES AND BITS

If I were the tech correspondent on a local morning news show talking to my audience of elderly ladies and Mr. Moms, I would advise them to "turn their paper into bytes (scan them) and then bits (shred them)!" Then I would probably hang myself at the commercial break. A screenwriter friend of mine by the name of John August talked me into scanning and tossing everything a couple of years ago and I've never looked back. Since John has scripts flying around every day, he tends to have more experience managing paper than most, so I listened to him (you should listen to him, too, on his INCREDIBLE advice-for-writers Web site, JohnAugust.com). Pretty much any scanner with an auto-feeder will work (using just a flatbed plate scanner to get one page at a time will suck the joy out of your brain). I use the Epson GT-S50 (they're not paying me, blah blah blah), which sails through twenty-five pages per minute. Dedicated document scanners are actually somewhat 'spensive ($200 to $500), but you can get one o' those printer/scanner/fax/copier jobbies for around $75. They're not amazeballs, but they WILL get the job done. Justify it this way: If there was a bunch of trash in your house and you could give a tiny wizard $75 to make it disappear, wouldn't you?? (You should also ask the tiny wizard for invincibility and more attractive genitals while he's there.)

Once scanned, I save each doc as a PDF with the following file nomenclature: [company name]_[type of doc]_[date]. If you're an example-phile, then here's how that might look: Allstate_auto_2011.10.23. (The date your file was created will be saved as metadata, but I like to include the year, month, and day in the name of the file so that I can "sort by name" in the file tree.) Not all documents come from companies, mind you, so you can do [type of doc]_[subject]_[date]. Let's say you're a contract killer hired to remove the czar of ancient Serbia. Your murder purchase order might look like this: Assassination_Czar_1346.5.30.

Next, it's off to the elimination box! Shredders are cheap and fun to use. You can imagine the screams of the documents that were sent to make your life worse as they go through the rotating death wheels. Destroy every piece of paper with your name and address on it that you don't need. Naturally SOME docs have to be kept as originals—birth certificates, legal notices, your mortgage or rental contracts, for example—so you can keep those in the traditional file-folder system. Currently it's not possible to remove ALL of the paper in your life, but the scan and shred can help you get rid of MOST of it.

Stop being a filthy hoarder. Take all the stuff you don't normally use and *trash it*. You will feel lighter and more in control. Think of it as "filing it into forever" or at least "wiping the excess poo off your brain's bum."

CHARACTERCIZE

 If you have the energy, make a note of all of your stuff.

 When you can see all of it on a page, it might be more apparent to you what you need to keep and what you can scrap.

LEARN TO SAY NO (BUT NOT TO THIS CHAPTER)

It's easy to identify the obvious time hijackers that wish to hamper your workflow when you need to get down to business—mindless web browsing, games, chatty neighbors—but sometimes you can get into a gray area in which things have the ability to disguise themselves as being helpful for your career. On their own, they might very well be, but in the context of the frenetic pace of your life, they actually run the risk of doing more damage than good. Recently I took on a side project that resulted in utter failure. I was brought in to lay down guide vocals for a film so that the actors would have tracks to choreograph their scenes to. I was given six days to learn ten songs that they wanted to record all in one day. That should have been my first *abort* clue, but sometimes I see red flags more as pretty decorations than as warnings that should be heeded. I was really busy working on a few other things, but I reasoned that I could learn the tracks in the car, mashed in between the cushions of my life.

THAT WAS A FAT SACK OF WRONG. The day came where I stood in a recording studio and proceeded to waste both hard drive space and tape (they were recording analog as well for some reason). Eight hours later, I left the studio with a kind of grime on my body that you almost convince yourself can only be scraped off with bark after you run your car into a tree. It's hard to admit to failing at something—failing people, their time, and yourself. But that's exactly what happened.

Fortunately, failure has a way of teaching valuable lessons.

Q: So where did I go wrong?
A: I never should have taken the project on to begin with.

I knew deep down that I was too busy to give it the attention it deserved, but the fat guy that is my ego sat right down on those doubts to silence their warning yaps. As a freelancer, it's very difficult for me to say no to things. Not only do I enjoy new challenges but there seems to be a script running in the root file system of my brain that says the only way to succeed is to always take on everything—after all, undertaking any work project is going to help get me the career I want, right??? I say no! Part of good time management involves not trying to force more variables into your time equation in the first place. Also I think Nerds have comic-book-inspired "hero syndrome," where we want to swoop in to the rescue so people like us can then tell other people, "Hey, that dude/lady is RAAAAAAD!" Then everyone high-fives you. Then Rodney Dangerfield shouts, "We're all gonna get laid!" and Kenny Loggins's "I'm Alright" plays as a gopher starts dancing. Needlesstosay, this is fallacious.

Taking on too much not only stresses you out more but eventually dips your energy scales into Diminishing Returns Land, a land where failure dragons swoop in and burn all the crops of your labor, and the saline content of the water supply causes your kidneys to harden because you are drinking from RIVERS OF YOUR OWN TEARS. In order for projects to help you flourish, you need to be the best "you" when doing them, and a frazzled you produces frazzled results across the board.

The trick to avoiding Diminishing Returns Land (again, this is an awful place: termites of impotency devour your chewy productivity centers from the inside out) is to stifle (or at least, ignore) the knee-jerk response to try to please everyone. When presented with a project, ask these three questions:

1. Is this in the wheelhouse of things I normally do?

NO!—Not a deal breaker, but definitely see questions 2 and 3.

YES!—Well, that's a start.

2. Would taking on this project REALLY change my life?

EH, NOT SO MUCH—The longer I live the more I find that it's rare that any one thing or job will change your life. Real, long-term success seems to be the aggregate sum of your tapestry of work.

DAMN SKIPPY!—You will know on a deep level if you're ultimately being offered the keys to a pile of success and better-looking sex mates.

3. As objectively as possible, do I really have the time to give this project the attention it deserves?

NEIN!—Then why are we still talking to ourselves about this? Do we have multiple personality disorder? Maybe we do . . . oh, shut up. No, YOU shut up!

YES, YES, A THOUSAND TIMES YES!—Then spread your wings and fly! Fly free, you delicious bastard!

I know, I know . . . we're all still basting in the affirmation juices of the 2008 film *Yes Man* (OK, I never saw it), but learning to be honest with people and say, "I would really love to take this on, but I'm afraid my current workload wouldn't provide me the time and energy to do your project the justice it deserves," will not only spare you the self-flagellation usually reserved for religious types but the job-offerers will also appreciate your sparing them a failure that could also affect *their* jobs. This also goes for the pro bono work that many of us freelancers do for our friends. It's good to help out others, but not at the expense of your mental health and career. You can use the aforementioned line. If they get mad at you anyway, well, then they're jagoffs. The other tasty side benefit to turning down work is that *it makes you more attractive.* Just like dating, people want what they can't have and not what's too available. It's like my good friend and successful manager Alex Murray always says: **"No is a very powerful word."**

CHARACTERCIZE

 Are you currently working on something you wish you had said no to?

 Write down the pain of the project to remind you to be more mindful of what you agree to next time.

BUILD YOUR WORKFOLIO

"Diversify!" That's what investment people always tell us. I think. I don't hang out with a lot of investment people. No particular reason. I'm sure they're all friendly and smell nice. The reasons for diversifying your stock portfolio are pretty obvious. It's the ol' "Don't throw all of your eggs in one basket" idea. It makes sense (unless you're literally a farmer with a basket fetish who strips nude while placing single eggs into fifty baskets—that is weird). Diversification makes sense and is a principle that should be applied to our work life. I firmly believe, especially in today's financial climate, it is IMPERATIVE to spin multiple plates. It's actually RISKIER to only have one job, as many people found out in the last few years. I'm not suggesting you run out and get a bunch of retail jobs. Instead, design a system and arrange your time so that it fills your soul as well as your bank account.

My work is the patchwork of a bunch of part-time jobs, all

sewn together to form a career. My jobs are able to form this unified career because they are all in the same business sector and revolve around one point of view. You certainly don't have to do that. You could work on a handful of completely disparate jobs, just because they interest you. The trick to this juggling act is that it's not a juggling act. You're not valuating each job equally. Instead, you're creating more of a Tetris board. You have the power to pick and choose the kinds of things you want to do and to decide with each job the level of compromise you're willing to make.

THE MALL ANALOGY

Despite its superficial facade and food court pizza odor, the American mall is actually a meticulously crafted organism. There are algorithms employed that predict that if, for a baseless example, you buy an ironic T-shirt from Hot Topic, you are likely to want those tiger-faced Ed Hardy Ugg boots as well. In light of this data, those two stores will be placed in close proximity to one another, making the separation of you from your money more facile. This particular example also MATHEMATICALLY proves you are a douche.

The point here is that in order to function smoothly and successfully, a mall has to have a good balance of stores that complement and support each other. This is an EXCELLENT model for your career. When designing your work life/career, try to look at the jobs you have or want as retail categories: large-chain department store, medium-sized shoe depot, and niche specialty shoppe.

DEPARTMENT STORE

This is the financial juggernaut that will anchor your business. It may be the heartless giant that keeps you afloat. You don't have to love this type of job, but you don't necessarily have to hate it either. As long as you recognize its role in your life, you might be more tolerant of its existence. Because you take this one for the cash, you should be willing to compromise creatively on it. Also it very well may consume the lion's share of your time. If it happens to be something that you love as well, then buy yourself a cake with the word "Huzzah!" written on it in red icing.

THE SHOE DEPOT

Shoe stores are usually midrange franchises that appeal to a wide variety of feet. The analogy here is that you need not devote as much time toward this job, and the pay is good but not amazing. If you are lacking a department store in your workscape, combining several shoe depots can help you maintain a comfy living.

NICHE SPECIALTY SHOPPE

The Pipe Store. A kite kiosk. A cart full of ceramic cat faces. These are the SUPERspecific products that represent VERY individual tastes. For your purposes, this is the passion project. A mall can't survive on these alone, but at least one of these is a MUST to keep your creative juices juicy. If your life is nothing but soulless survival work, YOU WILL DIE. Or at least, your soul will shrivel like a raisin and life will feel gray. Devote tidbits of time to your passion. Clock in for YOU. If this somehow blows up into your department store, purchase the aforementioned "Huzzah!" cake and a house made of candy.

CAPTURE THE MALL

"I fell off a carousel as a child, and the resulting surgery removed my ability to picture malls." How many times have you heard this excuse? Take a picture of your local mall's directory, print it out, and write over each of the store categories the jobs that you have or want. (Alternatively, you can make it a Charactercize and draw your own in your Character Tome.) This approach will not only help you generate work by forcing you to be specific, but it will also help you feel more in control of your destiny, which is, of course, to own everyone.

COMANAGING YOUR STORES

At the writing of this book, I'm also working on a handful of other projects and managing several stores at my mall: my current TV shows *Web Soup* and *Attack of the Show*, a network of podcasts, the Nerdist site, a Nerdist TV pilot, an animated TV pilot, a web interview show, two other TV shows I'm about to pitch, the setup of Nerdist Industries at Meltdown Comics, and stand-up (always with the stand-up). One simple concept has afforded me the opportunity to work on several projects at once, and if you care about creating a small empire in whatever field gives you brain-boners, you should tattoo it on your eyelids (side note: Do not actually tattoo this on your eyelids): COLLABO-RATE OR DELEGATE. That's it. That's the key to being a fancy multihyphenate. Collaborate with experts outside your area of knowledge or hire someone to work under you. It doesn't require a ton of money—collaboration is usually free and it is surprisingly inexpensive to pay someone on a freelance basis to cover things that would otherwise be dominating your time and spirit. Also it affords you the opportunity to learn about new areas of expertise. No cash? No problem! Partner with other folks and split the profits fifty-fifty. Are you experienced in a field? Take on an apprentice or intern! In return for his or her services you will provide valuable experience that will help them break into their chosen field.

As a self-centered only child, I was under the impression that, when it came to work, I had to do everything myself. (That is, in AD Chris Hardwick years, where AD = After Drinking.) Granted, there was a fair amount of control freakism at play, but I also thought there was greater glory in being the one-man band. There's a one-man band guy down at Santa Monica Pier. He has a guitar, and when he strums, it shakes a tambourine while the neck hits a symbol and his foot plays a kick drum. He doesn't seem like he feels too glorious. The truth is, if you try too hard to be doing EVERYTHING, you don't ever really focus on the most important thing, which should be the quality of your work. Kinda like one of those all-in-one printer/fax/scanners you got for the "Bytes and Bits" section. Sure, they do it all, but they don't really do any of it especially well. Their resources are spread thin and too focused on managing the energy required to cram a bunch of disparate things into one space rather than perfecting the output of any one job.

COLLABORATE FOR FUN AND PROFIT

Don't make the mistake of getting caught up in menial tasks you don't care about just because you have to be some kind of work martyr or control czar. Also don't waste trying to work in areas that are not your expertise (unless you really, really desire to learn a new skill). Collaboration opens you up to pretty much ANY field you've always wanted to try. Success in your life can come just as much from spotting talented people and forming partnerships. I'm not talking about seizing someone, exploiting their talents, and then taking credit for it—it's a two-way street. If you procure someone's services in a particular area you have to provide something in return. Very important life principle alert → **In order to get, you must first give.** That can be money or a split of the proceeds that may come from the final product, or teaching them about *your* thing. *Never forget that you yourself are a commodity.* If you are truly passionate and excited about what you are making, you will have an infectious quality that will inspire other humans to work with you to help you realize your—or a collective—vision. Examples!

WEB SOUP

- Collaborate with writing staff. (Easy one. This is a TV show with a production budget.)

ATTACK OF THE SHOW

- Same as above.

PODCASTS

- Teamed up with a couple of Nerds I found in an old arcade at a Greyhound station: Matt Mira and Jonah Ray.
- Podcast network: provide the production and delivery system for other people's shows.

ANIMATED SHOW

- Cowrote script with Mikes Henry and Phirman.
- Cowrote music with Phirman.
- Partnered with animation ninjas Puny Entertainment.

NERDIST INDUSTRIES

- Formed equity partnership with Geek Chic Daily.
  - » I provide creative content.
  - » They provide business infrastructure (they do all of that marketing, business-y stuff that used to pull me away from comedy-writing).

- Programming nightly live shows at NerdMelt.
  - » Hired theater director Emily Gordon to run the space.
  - » Paying her with revenue generated from shows.
  - » Brought on five interns who are gaining experience in production and comedy.

NERDIST TEES

- Teamed up with graphics Jedi Chris Glass.
  - » I send him ideas.
  - » He designs and fulfills orders at Wire and Twine.
  - » We split revenue.

THE NODE

- Teamed up with Red Magnet, a great social media company.
  - » They provide infrastructure, I provide content and promotion.
  - » Fifty-fifty partnership.

These are just a few ways that Nerds can mash their talents together to create things. This was the founding principle behind the Node—it was conceived to be a collaboration network for like-minded Nerds to inspire and help each other make things (http://node.nerdist.com). Ask yourself how your skills and talents could serve your partner; you should make it your task to find ways to complement those around you so everyone wins. I'm

SURE by now you must have written your skills and assets in your Character Tome, right? Maybe you should go back and check just to be sure. [winky emoticon]

CHARACTERCIZE

What types of things would you like to create but lack the skill?

Who do you know that might be able to collaborate with you?

If the above answer is "not a damn person," what are some ways you could find someone?

What can you offer in exchange?

YOUR GREATEST HITS

If you're going to shit on yourself when you fail, it is only right in the name of balance that you hug yourself when you succeed. Take the wins. Shut your eyes when they happen and just take a snapshot of the moment. FEEL what you have accomplished coursing through your veins. It is imperative that you start creating notches of appreciation for your efforts on your way to becoming someone who can manufacture goodness in the world.

In order to begin making any kind of improvements in my life I had to start writing stuff down. A complex writing system is our scepter next to the throne at the top of the food chain, so why not use it? You can laugh at your dog in a superior tone every time you do it. "Ha! I'm better at writing than you, Scott!" (My husky/Aussie shepherd mix's name is Scott.) As someone who tends toward being mercilessly hard on myself, I found that it was easy to let the "win" of successes vacate my conscious mind fairly quickly. I had a very "what have you done for me lately" relationship with myself, not unlike the hit song "What Have You Done for Me Lately?" by Ms. Jackson (because I'm nasty).

At the conclusion of each Julian calendar year, I would get into a headspace of "GAH! I didn't do ANYTHING this year. Still so far to go. So far . . ." Why it didn't occur to me until last year to actually take a personal inventory of moments is beyond me. (I'll beat myself up about that later, when you're gone.) After reading the previous section, I'm sure you tripped over your animals and family rushing to your computer to set up your simple color-coded calendar. This will be the log of your accomplishments. In fact, you can even create a specific color and calendar for "accomplishments" or "I'm rads" or whatever your internal dialect dictates. After you take any moment of victory, put it on the calendar at the time and day it happened. Sometimes jobs themselves are victories, so you don't need to make a redundant entry. December 31 or thereabouts, go ahead and make your "greatest hits of the year" list. If you don't like the album analogy, think of it as a growth chart, or those pencil notches your parents made on the wall as you got taller each year. It might feel a little weird, especially if you are uneasy accepting praise or aren't totally cool with blabbing about yourself, but don't worry—you don't have to show it to anyone and it's an important exercise in the paradigm shift of your relationship with yourself. Unless you write a book about it. #WhatHaveIDone

Here was mine from 2010:

TV
➤ *Web Soup*: 16 episodes
➤ *Attack of the Show*: 64 episodes

continued

- ➤ TV pilots: 5
- ➤ Talk show appearances: 23
- ➤ TV stand-up appearances: 4
- ➤ Did voice on new *Scooby Doo* where I got to say "I would have gotten away with it if it hadn't been for you meddling kids." (A lifelong dream! True story!)

Hard 'n Phirm
- ➤ Sold animated pilot to IFC
- ➤ Wrote *Benson Interruption* theme
- ➤ Did comedy show on Canadian TV
- ➤ Recorded with Weird Al (grade school me is still freaking out about it)
- ➤ Commercial campaigns: 2

Live Shows
- ➤ Comedy clubs: 11
- ➤ Other out-of-town shows: 5
- ➤ L.A. shows: 25
- ➤ Festivals: 6
- ➤ TOTAL SHOWS: 129
- ➤ Annual audience attendance improvement: ~200%

Nerdist Industries
Started Nerdist podcast!
- ➤ Episodes: 51
- ➤ Average downloads per episode by end of year: 100,000
- ➤ Had terrific guests (like the friggin' Muppets!)

Nerdist.com
- ➤ Traffic growth from previous year: 5 times
- ➤ Brought on contributors

➤ Hired Perry the editor
➤ Started Node social network

Publications
➤ Articles written for *Wired*: 2
➤ Smarmy self-help books sold to Penguin: 1

SIDE NOTE: There was some personal accomplishment stuff on here involving patience and relationships and the like, but I have to keep SOME things private. I encourage you to give your non-work-related milestones equal attention and weight. Did you lose your temper less? Were you caring to people at times? Selfless even? Note it.

Before I wrote this stuff down, I had thought 2010 was just an OK year, but I was reminded that I did actually get some stuff done. Sure, there was a bunch of stuff that didn't work out, but I don't focus on that beyond what I could learn from it. As you write, you will relive bits of those moments as you purge the forgotten triumphs from the recesses of your mental attic. It will feel good. The added bonus is that you may start trying to accomplish more in your life simply to be able to increase the list size, à la "RPG Your Life," so grab your Character Tome and get to work! The list should be proud, almost braggy. Like, it should feel slightly uncomfortable to show anyone—they'll think you have a penis on your back because you're patting yourself so much there. Kind of like how I feel right now . . .

CHARACTERCIZE

 Make your greatest hits list!

Like yourself more.

HOLESPOTTING!

As you develop your specific point of view, it's a good idea to get a bird's-eye view of the landscape of your chosen field. Who's doing what? Can you do it better? How could you do it differently? Look for the holes. When I started Nerdist a few years ago, I had this idea that there were comedy sites and there were tech sites but there wasn't really a composite of both. At least, not one that had my point of view. I felt like there might be a hole, or a unique skill set not being represented in the marketplace. Nerdist has grown out of its original concept of just covering tech, but it's the nature of things to evolve.

The more you can mash your specific interests into what you create, the better, because the less likely you are to have competition. If you only have one area of interest, there's a chance that many others have the same interest. Let's say you're a yarnsmith. (Everyone altogether, "*OK! YOU'RE A YARNSMITH!*") You've set up a li'l Etsy shop but are having trouble getting people to notice your generic designs. Does your work have a specific enough point of view? If your designs are abstract your challenge is going to be directing people to your page. What's your messaging? If you just have a sterile storefront and no real connections, you're counting on luck and the algorithm of Etsy's suggestion engine to make someone accidentally trip over your work. This is not impossible by any stretch of the imagination, but statistically it's a longer road. How could you make this more interesting? For starters, attach a story to your work. Give people an emotional hook to understand why you're doing what you're doing. As consumers, we love a good story. Don't lie or embellish, just tell your story and let people know who you are. Given two fake bread companies, which one are you more likely to buy from: (a) the bread manufactured by a large, faceless corporation, or (b) the bread that was made by a woman who was orphaned as a child and raised by a French bread maker in his live-in shop in Toulouse. Chances are, all things physical being equal, you're going to go for the emotional picture painted by the French lady.

Another question I asked myself when starting the Nerdist site was, "How can a site push through the din of the web?" At the time, Perez Hilton had just exploded and I was fascinated by it. There are TONS of gossip sites! Sure, he draws wieners and semen globs on pics, but SURELY there are other snarky entertainment news sites. Then I had a thought—it's him. The site is his name (albeit a pseudonym) and it has his face plastered on it. Other sites were just delivering news, something people have access to at all times. Perez's site read like he was your catty friend, and people naturally gravitated to that point of view, WAY more than the faceless machines of similarly themed sites. This approach was also more enticing for me because it afforded me the opportunity to connect with other Nerds on a personal level, which I have GREATLY enjoyed. As humans, we have a propensity for connection with other humans. (See *Twilight Zone*, episode 1, season 1, "Where Is Everybody.")

I had the extreme pleasure of hosting "W00tstock," the übershow of Wil Wheaton, Adam Savage, and Paul and Storm, one night while Wil was off working on *Eureka*. Dr. Demento was the special guest (my second favorite doctor), and while off to grab dinner after sound check, Phirm says to Demento, "Hey!

You wanna come get noodles with us?" to which he replied, "Sure!" So there we were at a Vietnamese noodle house on La Cienega Boulevard in L.A., sitting across from one of our childhood IDOLS while slurping cold vermicelli noodles and talking about legends of musical comedy (MUCH Tom Lehrer talk). Dr. D was telling us about his early days and how he came to be on the radio every week. It turns out he had an unmatchable knowledge for music. He also had more records than anyone. That's right, there was a time when possessing the physical content gave you the power. That's still sort of true today, but now people always have access to everything. It's not about necessarily just giving people content anymore. You now have to find interesting, point-of-view specific ways to deliver it. People want to relate to other people, not just consume soulless content. Put as much of you into your work as possible. Fortunately for me, Dr. D did both and my youth was filled with Weird Al, "Shaving Cream," and "Fish Heads."

YOU ARE NICHE

"Niche" used to be primarily one-dimensional. Now you almost have to measure the amount of content mashups with String Theory. Look for the crossroads of your interests to create a niche. Do you have any other interests besides yarn? YES! You also have a He-Man action figure collection and a fascination with the nineteenth-century philosopher Arthur Schopenhauer. Why not mash up all of your seemingly disparate interests into one thing? Personally, I would buy the SHIT out of a crochet tapestry of Beast Man's headshot over the phrase, "The universe is not a rational place." The more interests you have the better. Pull from all of your emotional sources to create a point of view the world hasn't seen before. In comedy we call this "finding your voice," and it is ESSENTIAL for success in the stand-up biz.

CHARACTERCIZE

 Write down holes—or specific areas not being serviced—in your field.

 Can you think of ways to fill one or more of them?

 What are all of your interests?

 Does mashing some of them together create a unique point of view?

 What's the story that got you to this POV?

 Write it down.

 Attach it to your niche.

MULTICASTING

"Multicasting" is a snazzy-sounding word that I co-opted for this book! In the computer world, it refers to sending a single transmission of data to a network of computers simultaneously. While you're juggling your various projects, oftentimes you can find clever ways to produce multiple results from a single source. Naturally, here's an example:

In the summer of 2010, I received an offer from my friends at Revision3, a great Nerd channel of web video content. They wanted to know if I was interested in interviewing Ozzy Osbourne for a show called *Digg Dialogg*. Yes! I was, in fact.

"Yowzers! He'd sure make a fanfuckingtastic podcast guest," I thought to myself out loud in the grocery store to the confusion of others at the deli meats counter. "But I'm sure he won't want me to interview him TWICE. Oh well . . ." "Wait, Brain!" I says. *"Digg Dialoggs* are edited down to twenty minutes . . . if I can sssssstttttttrrrrrreeeeettttttccccccchhhhhh the interview to forty-five, I can put out the unedited interview as a Nerdist podcast? Digg & Rev3 will get their shorter video and everyone gets something! I'll bet I could even squeeze a blog post out of it and a plug on *Attack of the Show!*" And that's what happened. Every outlet agreed, got the piece of the content that suited it, and I had stuff to put in four different places.

The key is to always look for opportunities and connections. Can you afford to take on various projects? Can your current slate of projects feed each other? If you have three projects feeding off of one source, you've just decreased your workload by roughly two-thirds and increased your income by who knows what. It's all about finding creative ways to engage your passions while repurposing content, but in a way that doesn't feel redundant. In fact, if you do it properly, the platforms should all complement each other. Hone your macro- and micro-focus skills—be aware of your big-picture surroundings to see what opportunities are available to you, and then be aware of the assets you have to fulfill them. If you can learn to do this, you will be an unstoppable T-1000 of productivity.

CHARACTERCIZE

 How can you dissect a project to disseminate it to different outlets?

What outlets are you currently servicing?

 Are there any you'd like to add?

Managing your time with calendar structure, constructive maintenance, and goal attainment should be a lifelong pursuit. As it yields more and more of the results you are looking for, it will feel less and less like work. You are now the designer of your life's game!

Congratulations! Give yourself another 50 XP points for completing this section!

RECURRING THEMES OF THIS BOOK

Whether intentional or unintentional or merely subconsciously intentional, there are a handful of recurring themes in this book besides penis jokes and swearing. I believe this handful of guiding principles can be applied to most anything, to the extent that if you feel lost or up against a creative wall, start with these basics to help get you over that first hump. (Tee hee—"first hump.")

MEASUREMENT

Data. The key to mastering anything is data. Lucky for YOU we live in a time when data is so easy to acquire. It should then be your pursuit to be an information gatherer. So much of the time I would find myself making choices and/or decisions based on assumptions that my brain was SURE were accurate. But how could they be? There was no real data. As previously stated, in the warmly titled *The 7 Habits of Highly Effective People*, Steven R. Covey postulates that we must "seek first to understand." His definition of this seems to be more in the way of listening to others blab on about their crap so we can see where they're coming from to make a mutually beneficial agreement. Being a science-liker, I interpret this maxim to also mean that we must listen to numbers and data so we can form a relationship with them. Through this empirical understanding, we are able to take this tangible information and manipulate it to suit our wants, needs, and goals.

Example time! I have a friend who was recently in the market for a new car via a trade-in. She asked for my advice. She was looking for a used car with low mileage, and possibly an SUV so she could cart her dogs all over the place. "What kind of car do you want?" I asked. "Well, I'm not sure. I like the Audi wagons, but the Cadillac SRX seems good, too. I just don't think I could afford either of them." "Really? How much are they?" "I'm not 100 percent sure." "OK, how much is your car worth?" "I dunno. Not too much, I think." "Have you taken your car into a dealer to see what they'd give you?" "No." "Have you gone onto the Blue Book site kbb.com to see AROUND what it is?" "No, I'm afraid to. What if it's way lower than I think it is?"

I know what you're thinking. This woman is not very bright. But that's not true! She's a supersmart lady-Nerd! I feel like this is not remotely uncommon. People form ideas based on assumptions and avoid actual info oftentimes for the same reason they don't like to go to the doctor for fear of getting "bad news." But I'm here to tell you that information is your salvation. Maybe her car is worth nothing and the Caddy is out of reach. BUT HOW DO YOU KNOW UNTIL YOU GET THE NUMBERS??? At least then you can formulate a plan. Information avoidance leaves you in this purgatory of inactivity because you're too afraid of the unknown. It'd be like never turning the lights on in your house and being too afraid to move because you don't want to trip over anything. Information gathering is flicking on the lights.

Be a scientist with your life. This is all they do! Measure, process, experiment, measure again, keep working until desired results are achieved. If Jonas Salk was all like, "I just don't know how much of the poliovirus I'd need to put in the vaccine . . . what if it's stupid?" WE'D ALL HAVE FUCKING POLIO. (Slight exaggeration with expletive assist for effect.)

Measure, manipulate. Quantify, modify. Track this, record that—time, weight, accomplishments, happy days—take a regular personal inventory. SPREADSHEET THAT SHIT. Pull data points onto the page so you can get a bird's-eye view of your life. Then give yourself numerical goals to shoot for. This is a major reason why video games can have a practical value: They teach us to keep score and aim higher next time. (This was never a valid argument to make to my parents when I was blowing off chores, of course, but it is a salient point.)

The secondary benefit to measuring where you ARE is tracking where you've BEEN. After a while you have accumulated data that you can go back and compare to the present day. You can even make graphs, dress your pets in ties, and give them a PowerPoint presentation on the performance of the product of YOU. If you do, please take video of it and send it to me at Chris Hardwick C/o Web Soup, 5750 Wilshire Boulevard, Los Angeles, CA 90036. In your presentation you will be able to experience undeniable proof of your progress. Focus on progress. Like Mayor Goldie Wilson. Progress is his middle name.

SERIOUSLY, JUST START

I get TONS of tweets and emails asking me how to "start" doing stand-up or "start" doing a podcast and my advice is always the same. You just start. There is no physical starting line, so it honestly doesn't occur to people that you could literally start something in an instant. THIS SECOND even. I guess it's a little weird because it feels a like a marathon with no physical starting line and all of a sudden some dude runs up, fires the starting gun, and shouts, "GO! GO! You're in a race now!!!"

That's all. No matter what you want to do, the only "thing" you have to do is stop thinking there is some magical barrier you have to cross. Currently YOU are the barrier, so stop being that for crapsake and just realize that you can start! If it's stand-up, look up open mikes and start going on stage. If it's podcasting, record on your phone if you have no other alternative. If it's something more academic, like architecture, that prevents you from doing it tonight, at least research what you need to do WHILE starting your own designs. Whatever it is, you have to STOP convincing yourself that it's dumb or gonna suck or that there's some giant thing you need to do first to "start." JUST FUCKING DO IT. No more excuses. Every minute you're not pursuing a creative passion in some capacity, be it hobby or career, you are wasting valuable time on this planet.

I do a ton of crowd work in my live shows and once chatted with a dude who said he was a law clerk, a job he loathed. When I asked what he wanted to do, he replied, "Publish web comics." "Have you published anything yet?" "Naw." "You know you can just PUT stuff on the Internet, right? There's no gatekeeper. You can put it there and then people can see it." "I know, I just . . . haven't . . . I'm trying to figure out how to start it." Start it. It's OK if it sucks at first, you'll get better. And it may not! It might be nine kinds o' radtacular right off the bat! It was weird how my podcast didn't feel real to me because it was a thing I actually liked doing and didn't materialize as an offer from a large, organized entity. I can tell you after a year and a half of doing it that it IS a real thing, and your passion is, too.

ENJOY THE PROCESS

Some people are annoyed by this phrase and even say it sarcastically when times get tough, but I think it's the only way to live. Goals are a great target for building our treasure maps, but the goal attainment moment is often brief and weirdly unsatisfying. This is because our biological nature tells us to grow. Once we harvest, the growth is over. That doesn't mean "never achieve your goals"; it means always look ahead to other growth. Achieve, be grateful, move on. This is why process is more important than goal attainment itself. *It's not about reaching a goal; it's about what you become in the process.* I get shit for saying the "process" on my podcast so much, but I don't give a care. Process is where the meat is. That's where you learn, where you grow. Always think "process, process, PROGRESS." Just don't say that out loud or someone might strike you.

Will you fall sometimes? OF COURSE you will. It's a valuable part of the PROCESS. Embrace it. If you're able to build from your falls you'll be unstoppable and damn near fearless. You see, every time you fall down and get back up, you add another piece of body armor to yourself. You learn what not to do, how to do better, and how to create comfort through practice. It's the only way to improve and it is ENTIRELY worth it. Trainer Tom had one of the coolest metaphors for life that I have ever heard. It made me suspicious that he might be an elderly

Asian master in a younger white guy suit. It was an idea along these lines: You are a fountain. Your only job is to shoot out water. You cannot control where the water goes. Sometimes it's into a good place, sometimes not. It doesn't matter. All you have to do in life is focus on keeping the water flowing.

I mean, C'MOWN!!!! Even as much of a cynical D-bag as I can be, that idea got to me in a "I felt my soul twitch" kind of way. That is some good stuff. Keep the water flowing with creation, my little fountains.

GO EASY ON YOURSELF

As a subclass of humans, Nerds are excruciatingly critical. You will see this if you've ever been on a Nerd's hunting ground, the message board. Unfortunately, the person a Nerd tends to be hardest on is himself or herself. I know this because I do it. And all of my Nerd friends do it. I IMPLORE you to go easy on yourself. Seriously. This world is challenging enough without adding the obstacle of self-loathing. Being constructively critical is good, as long as your purpose is to improve your methods for future endeavors. Lying in bed and replaying failures and telling yourself you're stupid is a tremendous disservice to your efforts and what you can offer the world.

Here's another version of this, wrapped in a nice li'l bow of insecurity: You're hanging out with someone you like and/or respect. You make a comment about something. On your way home, you play back the night in full-mental HD, and your brain flags the comment. As you loop it over and over again you are convinced that you offended the person because your comment could have been easily misconstrued. After several hours or a night of torturing yourself, you reach out to the person to apologize for the comment. They usually respond with a "Oh, I didn't take it that way! No problem!" You feel better, the pattern repeats the next night. I get it! You want people to like you and you don't want to offend them and give them a reason not to. Here's how I got over this → First off, you're most likely not a dick and unless you overtly insult someone's grandmother you probably didn't come off the way you think you did. Second, if you are genuinely committed to being more comfortable with who you are, being worried at every turn what people think about you won't matter. Last, and most crucial, I realized that the second you're not standing in front of someone, they're not thinking about you anymore. Your concern over how someone took your probably benign comment is a very self-centered point of view. You think you're still affecting that person. The good news is, the overwhelming chance is that that person is just as self-centered and is probably thinking about himself or herself and NOT YOU. They were probably even doing this while you were "offending" them and wouldn't be able to repeat the conversation back to you if asked.

SIDE NOTE TO "HONEST" PEOPLE—PET PEEVE ALERT: Please do not use this as a license to express whatever you feel like guilt-free. Surely you know some hateful twat who offers their negative, unsolicited opinion about you to your face: "Your shirt's dumb," and when you slightly protest they fire back with, "Hey, I'm just an honest person. That's who I am. Sorry if you can't handle that." Here's my message to these people, "FUCK YOU. A LOT. FOREVER." "Honest" people give a truthful assessment when asked. "Douche bags" say any old shitty thing to people whenever they feel like. They presuppose that anyone gives a shit about their useless opining. (SEE

SHIFT YOUR INCREDIBLE FOCUS

One-Minute Hugs

Even if everything's going to shit and your favorite pastime is punching yourself in the balls (ladies have balls, too; they're just all hidden up inside—BUT I'M GONNA FIND 'EM!!!) because you feel like you deserve inordinate amounts of abuse, just try this thing I'm about to tell you: Like yourself for one minute a day. Just a minute. The other 23:59 you can bathe in self-loathing's brownish glow.

Time it so you don't like yourself too much, because that could be disastrous. If you start to like yourself, you would start to radiate happiness and confidence. Then people might try to start conversations with you and WHAT A PAIN. Friends are overrated—always being there for support and shit. Making you feel warm and loved. Fuck that. No, you only get a minute.

Close your eyes and think of something you did that was good. Appreciate something about yourself. "BUT THERE'S NOTHING . . ." Bullshit. There's something that can fill a minute. Even if you screwed up a thing maybe you screwed up less than yesterday. Remember, the fact that you even read this far because you were curious to find answers to help yourself means that you are on the right path.

I'm not saying I have all the answers. In fact, I'm a narcissistic assjob who clearly has untamably huge balls for even daring to write a book of this nature. (I can say this about myself because this isn't my minute.) If you are someone who would enjoy receiving one-, two-, or even FIVE-MINUTE HUGS from other creatures in your species, then you need to lead by example. If you can learn to not always rely on outside forces to hug your insecurities away because YOU are able to do it FIRST, you will be virtually invincible (except to things like poison and bullets). If the one thing that you take away from this book is that you cultivate the gift of being kind and respectful to yourself, your money will have been well spent.

THE NERDIST WAY   269

Douche bag/robot connection, page 17.) When faced with these hate-demons, you may politely and smugly respond with, "Awwww, that's ADORABLE that you think your unsolicited opinion means anything to anyone! I just wanna pinch your odious little cheeks and wrap you in a blanket. Like a house pet!"

It's very easy to attack ourselves. Even comforting in its familiarity, but you must resist this urge at all costs. Dwelling on the past or your perceived flaws will do nothing but keep you under emotional house arrest and hamper your progress. Commit yourself to growth and reward yourself with kindness for choosing to do so!

YOU. ARE. WORTH. IT.

When I first landed this book deal, I crapped a little bit because I honestly hadn't thought past the proposal. What hadn't occurred to me before was that, if the book sold, I would actually have to write it. Everyone told me it would be a miserable process. "You'll BEG to give the money back just to make it go away," one comic said. This was never the case. The writing of this book has been one of the most pleasurable and rewarding experiences of my life. Writing a book isn't that hard, honestly. It just takes an outline and a little discipline. Building off the thirty-four page proposal, I listed sections and chapters I thought would comprise the manuscript. Then I started writing around the middle of December, here and there, whenever I could. And that's it. If you have an idea and an outline, you could write a book in about three and a half months writing five hundred words a day on weekdays. It won't feel overwhelming when you break it down into small chunks like that. Five hundred words is just a few paragraphs. And you can always go back and change it later if you don't love the first pass. The important things are to DECIDE and START. Then stay committed until you're done.

I'm not special or particularly smarter than you or anyone else. I just figured out who I am and came up with a plan. I love that movie *The Edge* with Anthony Hopkins and Alec Baldwin. One line always stuck in my head because Sir Anthony's character, billionaire Charles Morse, spouts this catchphrase throughout the film: "What one man can do, another can do!" YOU are that "another," so go out and fucking DO IT. (But you don't have to kill a bear with a stick, like Morse.)

You deserve every wonderful thing you want in this life. There is no merit in toiling in a sadness dungeon. Work hard and play nicely. We have a saying on the Nerdist podcast: ENJOY YOUR BURRITO. It was born on episode 39 with Rainn Wilson. Lovable Nerdist sidekick Jonah Ray explained that when his life was shitty, his only joy was this one burrito from a Mexican food shack near his apartment. Halfway through the burrito, he'd get depressed because he knew it would soon be over. One day he decided to "enjoy the burrito"—in other words, live in the present and appreciate something good while it was happening. At the end of the ep, I think it may have been Rainn who signed off with "Enjoy your burrito, people." We liked the message and have been signing off that way ever since. And so, I thank you for reading this book and letting me blab about myself and what I think about stuff. I sincerely hope the lessons I learned through a young lifetime of mistakes were helpful to you at least a little bit as you aim for that next level. While navigating this world, use your obsessively Nerdy brain to focus on things like looking for opportunities, dissecting your failures for lessons, and committing yourself to the emotional rewards and happiness you absolutely deserve for being an intelligent, empathetic human being.

ENJOY YOUR BURRITO!

NERDIST ORIGIN STORY

When you first start working in television, you pretty much have the mind-set that you have to take any old job that comes around. Jobs are precious, and you don't have the luxury to wait around for something you really *want* to do.

OR DO YOU???

In 2007, work was slow. I was starting to get antsy. "I'm still doing the right thing here, being in this business, right??" I would silently ask myself numerous times a day. The life of a freelancer can be stressful, as you may well know. Even if I had a job, I always felt the tug of anxiety about the prospects (or lack thereof) for the next one. I had my shit pretty much together but no direction. I was getting frustrated just waiting for work to fall into my lap. Performing stand-up a few nights a week gave me the sense that I was moving forward, but comedy in L.A. pays zero dollars, so it was "for the love of the craft" type work. Mike

Phirman and I had gotten news that we would tape our Comedy Central half-hour special later that year, but beyond that there wasn't much else to talk about workwise. I started having daily freak-outs about my future.

One night in July while trying to swat away stress mosquitoes that were preventing my sleep, something snapped. I had felt pushed up against a wall and I was tired of living that way. Living through a fear filter is a horrible life. It's hard to make good decisions when you're in fear mode, because your main goal is usually to run around in circles while covering your head from the plummeting sky. For the preservation of my sanity, it would have to end. I decided that I was going to figure out the career thing, no matter what. I just was. There wasn't a failure option. I don't know where I was drawing this assurance and confidence from, but it felt better than the shit-cage I had imprisoned myself in for so long. I slept well that night. I dreamed I had organic web-shooters (unnecessary side note).

The next morning I woke up and had an epiphany: I needed to pursue work that involved my passions. This seemingly obvious realization felt so revolutionary to me. Why had it NEVER occurred to me to do this before? I loved tech, science, math, comedy . . . I could do something with that! Between the web and five hundred channels of television, certainly a career in the Nerd sector could happen now, where this type of niche (by TV standards) programming wouldn't have existed even just ten years prior. I reasoned that I had tons of hosting experience, and mashing that up with comedy and sci/tech would create a space that I felt was new. I also felt that no one would be better at this than me (I was feeling oddly cocky). I would find this job, build a career around it, and only take jobs that revolved around the Nerdsphere.

I immediately called my manager, Alex, one of the smartest, nicest, and most level-headed dudes I know. He was supportive without pandering, but when I excitedly told him my plan I sensed a slight, "O . . . K . . . we can try on that . . ." It's a weird thing for a client who isn't working and has no power to dictate the jobs he was and wasn't going to take, but Alex went along with it. My resolution was getting stronger.

I SWEAR TO THE GODS a handful of days later I was surfing the job breakdowns for the entertainment biz (technically something I wasn't supposed to be doing) because I was in a "grab stuff by the ballbags" frame of mind and stumbled across a listing for a science show that *Wired* magazine was producing for PBS. They were looking for a host. I almost couldn't believe what I was reading. Now, I can't say I've read *The Secret* or anything, but this was some crazy *Secret* shit if I had ever seen it. This seemed to be, top to bottom, EXACTLY what I wanted to do. I called Alex and spewed out a "holyshitpantsyougottagetmeanauditionforthisshow" kind of run-on.

He got me an audition and the next week I was driving onto the KCET lot—the local PBS affiliate who would serve as the production studio—in Silver Lake. BTW, KCET was exactly what you'd think: a movie studio facility that dated back to 1912, and while expansions and improvements had been made, the original structures still stood in the middle of it. Also, the rest of the buildings had gone relatively unchanged since the '70s, complete with fantastic brown furniture and wall art. If Mr. Rogers had had a compound, this was it.

Three auditions later I had the job. *Wired Science* was a phenomenal experience. I got to work with nice, SUPERsmart people. Way smarter than myself or anyone I had worked with in the past. The show only lasted ten episodes and remnants of it still populate the far corners of the Internet. But I quickly became friends with all of the *Wired* staffers pulling double duty to work on the TV show: Melanie Cornwell (head of special projects), Scott Dadich (creative director), and Adam Rogers (senior editor). This show was the undeniable catalyst for everything I have going on currently. It led to a writing gig for *Wired* mag, and though its exposure was limited, it caught the eye of G4 TV, which had just lost a terrific gadget reviewer by the name of Will O'Neill on *Attack of the Show*. The timing was perfect. Like a glob of alabaster caulk, I filled the position in December of that year.

In August 2008, I wanted to expand. I had had a personal blog on TypePad but rarely updated it. I loved sites like Gizmodo and Lifehacker, so I decided to create a blog that was mostly about other things, but delivered through my point of view. I wanted the idea that Nerds now owned pop culture to be an ideology to which anyone could subscribe, therefore the "ism" of it all. ("I HATE isms," I heard Ferris Bueller say in my head.) Magically, Nerdist.com was available.

Since that time, Nerdist has sprouted a bunch of different heads, between a podcast, a book, and a television show, but it's all pieces of the same voice, which is mine. In Sir Richard Branson's book *Business Stripped Bare*, he talks about how people chastised him early on for daring to suggest that Virgin could expand into areas beyond music. To paraphrase, "It wasn't the product," he would tell them. "It was the Virgin experience." The important factor was that the point of view was consistent whether it was a record label, an airline, a train, or a mobile carrier. He's done pretty well with that philosophy and it's something that I think, as content creators, we should all strive for.

I've never been happier or prouder with my work than with

Nerdist Industries. It is fulfilling in ways I never could have postulated, because I have ownership over it—not just legally, but creatively. To get paid to create things that interest you is one of the greatest gifts you can receive, and I highly recommend it. I am living proof that it is possible.

I thank you! You finished the whole book! Even the last jerk-offy part where I congratulate the shit out of myself! Just for that, give yourself additional 100 XP and a bunch of high-fives!!!

PS—You're nice!

THANK YOU

THANK YOU THANK YOU THANK YOU **BERKLEY BOOKS** THANK YOU THANK YOU **THE PENGUIN GROUP** THANK YOU THANK YOU **ALEX MURRAY** THANK YOU THANK YOU THANK YOU THANK YOU **HANNAH GORDON** THANK YOU THANK YOU **ANDIE AVILA** THANK YOU **PAM BARRICKLOW** THANK YOU THANK YOU THANK YOU **ADAM ROGERS** THANK YOU **MOM (SHARON HILLS)** THANK YOU **JIM HILLS** THANK YOU THANK YOU **JIM FACENTE** THANK YOU THANK YOU THANK YOU **DAD (BILLY HARDWICK)** THANK YOU THANK YOU THANK YOU THANK YOU **MIKE PHIRMAN** THANK YOU **JONAH RAY** THANK YOU **MATT MIRA** THANK YOU THANK YOU THANK YOU THANK YOU THANK YOU **JANET VARNEY** THANK YOU THANK YOU **ROB ZOMBIE** THANK YOU THANK YOU **CRAIG FERGUSON** THANK YOU **TOM DETERS** THANK YOU THANK YOU **TONI DETERS** THANK YOU **PETER LEVIN** THANK YOU **CHRIS GLASS** THANK YOU **PERRY MICHAEL SIMON** THANK YOU THANK YOU **CHAD CHRISTOPHER** THANK YOU THANK YOU **LAUREN GREGG** THANK YOU THANK YOU **STEVE MARTIN** THANK YOU THANK YOU THANK YOU THANK YOU **CHAI LATTES** THANK YOU THANK YOU THANK YOU **DOCTOR WHO** THANK YOU THANK YOU THANK YOU THANK YOU **SALT & VINEGAR CHIPS**

THANK YOU

Software Used

Scrivener for book writing—literatureandlatte.com

Dropbox for file syncing—dropbox.com

Evernote for note-taking (heavy-lifting)—evernote.com

Plaintext for note-taking (low impact)—hogbaysoftware.com

Epic Win for ToDo-listing—www.rexbox.co.uk/epicwin

iCal for calendaring—me.com

Gmail for emailing—gmail.com

Firefox for browsing—firefox.com

Cyberduck for FTPing—cyberduck.com

Libsyn for podcast hosting—libsyn.com

Tweetdeck for tweeting (desktop)—tweetdeck.com

Twitter for tweeting (iOS)—twitter.com/download

Parallels on Mac for PCing—parallels.com

Quicken Home & Business 2011 for money tracking—intuit.com